every dog has a gift

every dog has a gift

True Stories of Dogs
Who Bring Hope & Healing
Into Our Lives

Rachel McPherson

FOUNDER AND EXECUTIVE DIRECTOR,
THE GOOD DOG FOUNDATION

with Deborah Mitchell

JEREMY P. TARCHER/PENGUIN
a member of Penguin Group USA, Inc.
New York
A Lynn Sonberg Book

JEREMY P. TARCHER/PENGUIN
Published by the Penguin Group
Penguin Group (USA) Inc., 375 Hudson Street, New York, New York 10014, USA •
Penguin Group (Canada), 90 Eglinton Avenue East, Suite 700, Toronto, Ontario M4P 2Y3, Canada
(a division of Pearson Penguin Canada Inc.) • Penguin Books Ltd, 80 Strand, London WC2R 0RL, England •
Penguin Ireland, 25 St Stephen's Green, Dublin 2, Ireland (a division of Penguin Books Ltd) • Penguin Group
(Australia), 250 Camberwell Road, Camberwell, Victoria 3124, Australia (a division of Pearson Australia Group
Pty Ltd) • Penguin Books India Pvt Ltd, 11 Community Centre, Panchsheel Park, New Delhi–110 017, India •
Penguin Group (NZ), 67 Apollo Drive, Rosedale, North Shore 0632, New Zealand (a division of Pearson
New Zealand Ltd) • Penguin Books (South Africa) (Pty) Ltd, 24 Sturdee Avenue, Rosebank,
Johannesburg 2196, South Africa

Penguin Books Ltd, Registered Offices: 80 Strand, London WC2R 0RL, England

First trade paperback edition 2011
Copyright © 2010 by Rachel McPherson and Lynn Sonberg
All rights reserved. No part of this book may be reproduced, scanned, or distributed
in any printed or electronic form without permission. Please do not participate
in or encourage piracy of copyrighted materials in violation of the authors' rights.
Purchase only authorized editions.
Published simultaneously in Canada

Most Tarcher/Penguin books are available at special quantity discounts for bulk purchase for sales promotions,
premiums, fund-raising, and educational needs. Special books or book excerpts also can be created to fit specific
needs. For details, write Penguin Group (USA) Inc. Special Markets, 375 Hudson Street, New York, NY 10014.

The Library of Congress catalogued the hardcover edition as follows:

McPherson, Rachel.
Every dog has a gift : true stories of dogs who bring hope & healing into our lives / Rachel McPherson
with Deborah Mitchell.
p.   cm.
Includes index.
ISBN 978-1-58542-795-6
1. Animals as aids for people with disabilities.   2. Dogs—Therapeutic use.   3. Working dogs.
4. Human-animal relationships.   I. Mitchell, Deborah R.   II. Title.
HV1569.6.M37   2010   2009048776
362.4'0483—dc22

ISBN 978-1-58542-899-1 (paperback edition)

Printed in the United States of America
1   3   5   7   9   10   8   6   4   2

This book is printed on acid-free paper. ∞

BOOK DESIGN BY AMANDA DEWEY

Some of the names and identifying characteristics have been changed to protect the privacy of the individuals
involved.

While the authors have made every effort to provide accurate telephone numbers and Internet addresses at the time
of publication, neither the publisher nor the authors assume any responsibility for errors, or for changes that occur
after publication. Further, the publisher does not have any control over and does not assume any responsibility for
author or third-party websites or their content.

To all the dogs who share their special gifts
and help humans heal

CONTENTS

2.

dogs that change lives

3.

kids + dogs = magic

4.

getting involved

INTRODUCTION

In a way, the seeds of this book have been lying dormant for many years. Ever since I was a young child, dogs have been an important and influential part of my life. My passionate belief in the transformational power of the human/dog relationship came to a head in an exciting way about a decade ago when I founded and became executive director of The Good Dog Foundation, a nonprofit organization that is dedicated to all aspects of dog-assisted therapy. Good Dogs bring comfort and joy to people receiving chemotherapy, restore a sense of control to people whose lives have been upended by an illness or disability, serve as the perfect audience to help disadvantaged children practice and improve reading skills, comfort the bereaved and victims of disasters, and much more.

When I founded The Good Dog Foundation, I was bursting with enthusiasm, and today I am reinvigorated daily with the ideas, challenges, joys, and love that come from working with all the terrific dogs, volunteers, staff, and clients of the Foundation. Now I feel it is time for me to share some of the incredibly special moments and stories surrounding the relationship between people and dogs that have blessed and enriched my own life over the years.

First, I want to emphasize my firm belief that each and every dog is a therapy dog. That's not to say that every dog has gone through a specially designed training program so he or she can behave appropriately in a clinical setting. I'm saying that all dogs inherently have the power to heal, and they all want to give love and to be loved in return, even those who appear to act frightened or vicious. And what better therapy is there than love?

In this book we hope to illustrate the power, magnitude, and magic of that love as told in stories that inspire and move readers. I say "we" because without the cooperation of the volunteers and staff at The Good Dog

Foundation, the people who have been the recipients of Good Dog visits, and people from all walks of life across the country who have shared their special dog stories with me—and of course the dogs themselves—this book would not have been possible.

Make no mistake . . . this is not "just" a collection of stories about dogs. I have found that when you are dealing with the relationship between dogs and people, the stories go much deeper and stir up more primal, universal emotions. Although we have attempted to group the stories in this book by theme—healing and teaching life-changing situations, and the special relationships dogs have with children—we know these divisions are artificial and that every life story straddles several domains. Still, it is our hope that these categories may provoke readers to gain a new perspective or open up possibilities for expanding their own relationships with their canine companions.

With that concept in mind, I have also included a section with practical information, called "Closing Tails," at the end of each section. Each of these sections offers readers a variety of practical information that ties in with the part's main theme, including, for instance, activities parents and their children can engage in with their dogs at home; training tips; information on volunteer opportunities; contact information on organizations that provide therapy dogs, service dogs, and search-and-rescue dogs; and suggested reading materials.

My goal in sharing these stories and related activities is to help people become more engaged in the relationship they have with dogs and to help them enhance that relationship for themselves and beyond, into the lives of their family, friends, colleagues, and others in the community. My hope is that the stories in this book will not only make people stop and think about dogs in a different way but also introduce them to some of the many constructive, loving, and joyful opportunities there are to interact with dogs in their daily lives.

Why I Wanted to Write This Book

As a child growing up in Mississippi, I understood intuitively that dogs can play critical roles in our lives. I know it was true for me. I have a sister, Ann, who is fifteen years my senior, and I looked up to her. When I was about three years old, Ann went away to college. I was crushed and filled with a great sense of loss. My salvation was Uncle Bud: a French bulldog who became my constant compan-

*Rachel McPherson and Good Dog Fidel visiting with Alice
at Gilda's Club in Manhattan. The Good Dog Foundation
makes regular visits to Gilda's Club to meet with kids
whose lives have been affected by cancer.*

ion and confidant. When Uncle Bud was stolen, I felt as
if my best friend had been taken away—again. Shortly
thereafter our family adopted a standard poodle, Fifi,
and from then on, all through my teen years and college,
and as I entered the work world, dogs continued to be a
part of my life. And then a shift occurred.

I was working as a producer for film and television
with my own company, Southern Voices, which produced

dramatic adaptations of southern literature, among other endeavors. In 1984, one of my documentaries, *Signals Through the Flames*, was nominated for an Academy Award in the best documentary film category. In the mid 1990s, in preparation for a documentary that would feature therapy dogs, I began to conduct nationwide research on therapy dogs and the work they do. Although I thought I was already a passionate dog person, I was soon to discover new depths to the incredibly positive impact that one-on-one interactions between people and dogs can have, not only on the direct participants in such relationships, but on close family and friends. I became fascinated with therapy dogs and the healing powers that seemed to magically take hold when an ailing, dying, emotionally distraught, physically challenged, or otherwise hurting or traumatized individual was paired with a therapy dog.

In the midst of my research I learned that it was against the law to take dogs into a hospital in New York. To me, this was an absolute outrage. Here we had the means to bring comfort, joy, pain relief, and love to people in need, essentially without cost or risk of drug-related side effects, and patients were being denied that care. I knew I had to do something. That something grew into several projects, but none of them included the documentary.

Rather than do a film on the subject, I decided to devote my energy to creating The Good Dog Foundation, which was founded in 1998, and changing the law that barred therapy dogs from visiting hospitals and other health care facilities. We succeeded on both counts, and today Good Dogs make more than 260,000 visits to people in health care, social services, and community organizations and schools in New York, New Jersey, Massachusetts, and Connecticut each year. After the work that Good Dogs did at Ground Zero helping the families of victims of 9/11, The Good Dog Foundation created a disaster-response training course for its volunteers. Because of that training, Good Dogs were enlisted by the Mississippi Department of Mental Health to assist families after Hurricane Katrina. The Good Dog Foundation has been honored on the floor of the Westminster Kennel Club Dog Show because of its work with Hurricane Katrina survivors, and has received awards from the American Society for the Prevention of Cruelty to Animals (ASPCA) and the American Red Cross for its work in New York City in the aftermath of the September 11 attacks.

All the accolades in the world cannot take the place of the satisfaction I get from working with Good Dogs—and all dogs—and seeing the joy, healing, and love that occur and blossom when dogs and people interact. This book is just one way to share that satisfaction, and I want to offer it to the world.

1

dogs as healers
and teachers

A Gift for Milo

In February 2009, Claire sent an unusual package
from New York City to Lake Oswego, Oregon: her
eleven-year-old son's dirty sweatshirt. The soiled
garment went with the following note: "This is Milo's
shirt, for Chad." Chad would be sleeping with the shirt
until he got to meet its owner a few weeks later, after jet-
ting across the United States.

The gift makes more sense when you learn that it is
for Milo's future service dog, trained by Autism Service
Dogs of America (ASDA). This nonprofit organization

provides uniquely trained service dogs for children who have autism and their families.

The sweatshirt with Milo's scent allows Chad to become acquainted with his new friend before they actually meet. The story began eighteen months earlier, when Claire contacted the ASDA about getting help for her son, who is seriously debilitated with autism.

"The whole long process has been one of enormous hope," says Claire. "I try to stay focused and just take each day as it comes."

Indeed, taking one day at a time has been the way of life for Claire, a single mom, and her two sons, Milo and Sasha. Finding the right schools for her son has been difficult. He has been in and out of special education classes and, at one point, his problems were so severe that he needed to be hospitalized for six months in an inpatient psychiatric unit specializing in autism spectrum disorders at Bellevue Hospital in New York City.

At the age of seven, Milo began attending Green Chimneys, a special residential school in upstate New York just a short distance from New York City, and Claire was happy to see some progress during the two years Milo was there: He learned how to read and seemed to focus

Left to right: *Sasha, Chad, and Milo*

better. He also developed a great affinity for animals, as the school includes working with animals as part of its therapy program . . . an experience that paved the way for his future relationship with Chad.

But when Milo was nine, Claire decided she wanted him to live at home and attend public school in New York City. Unfortunately there was no room for Milo; all of the public school autism programs were overenrolled. Frustrated by her inability to get her son the help he needed, Claire got the idea to apply for a service dog specially trained to work with autistic children. Her hope was that Milo could attend a regular public school with Chad to help him through the day.

The program where Chad was trained is in Oregon, and the process of applying for the dog was complex. Among other things, Claire had to prepare a video of her son to submit to the school where the service dogs were trained. And with the help of dozens of friends, relatives, and other caring individuals, Claire raised the $13,500 needed to get Chad. Then the waiting began.

The eighteen-month wait for Chad seemed interminably long at times, but Claire focused on preparing Milo for the new addition to his world. She talked about the dog often, reinforcing for Milo that Chad was coming especially for him and that they would be able to share good times every day. Although Milo was excited and happy that Chad was coming, he could not verbalize how he felt because it was a new experience, and new experiences made Milo very anxious.

One way Milo expresses his anxiety and his struggles with everyday life is to shout. In fact, it is common for Milo to wake up yelling every morning, which is simply his way of letting out some of the anxiety he is feeling. It is also common for Milo to become upset in stressful situations. One day Claire decided to take Milo and Sasha shopping. When they got out of the cab, Milo accidentally bumped the side of a Lexus with the cab door. The owner of the Lexus jumped out of his car and yelled at Milo, and Milo started to run. Claire was torn between trying to explain to the man that Milo was ill and didn't mean to bump the car and trying to watch where Milo was going. Fortunately, Milo didn't get too far and Claire was able to catch up with him. Yet, for the next hour or so, Milo was in "meltdown" mode, yelling and out of control.

"If we had had a service dog, it would have communicated to the owner of the Lexus that we had a special situation," says Claire, "and there would have been a better understanding. The dog also could have been a source of calm and comfort for Milo."

Finally it was time for Claire to fly to Oregon to become acquainted with Chad. During her stay Claire learned how to interact with and handle the dog so she could pass the ASDA's required tests before bringing Chad home. From the moment Chad and Milo got together, Claire has been amazed at the positive changes in her son that have taken place. And they just keep getting better.

"Milo has been much more talkative, which is a huge difference. In fact, he's downright chatty. He loves telling me all kinds of anecdotes and he does it all with this very happy smile on his face," says Claire. "Milo has always loved history, and since Chad arrived, he is absolutely eager to share what he's learned that he finds interesting. Just the other night he started telling me a very long story about King George! He can actually stay focused and remember so many details. This is completely different from the way he was before Chad came."

In the past, Milo's inability to deal with changes in his environment typically meant that he screamed and thrashed about, but Claire has seen a change in this behavior as well. "For example, Milo fell in the kitchen a few weeks after Chad arrived. In previous times, Milo would have spent at least fifteen minutes shouting and thrashing because he is hypersensitive to even minor pain. I braced myself for this typical reaction. To my surprise, he reached for Chad, who was by his side, and spent two minutes hugging and kissing the dog! And that was the end of the incident. Similar scenarios have occurred since Chad arrived, and Milo has reacted with the same kissing behavior. It is truly amazing."

The bonding that happened between Milo and Chad

Chad and Milo

seemed almost immediate, Claire explains: "Milo loves to take care of Chad. He takes his responsibility very seriously and spends lots of time petting and sitting with the dog. Whenever Milo needs comforting, and he often does, he goes to Chad."

Claire has also noticed the positive impact these changes in Milo have had on how they all live together as a family.

"Sasha, his older brother, is thrilled to have Chad here as well. He has had to be almost a 'service brother' for Milo for so long, and now he can have some space of his own."

Recently, in an essay he wrote for admission into high school about his experience having a brother with autism, Sasha wrote that Chad "helps my brother in ways I cannot put into words. I'd probably use the word 'miracle.' He calms him down so much that you would think Milo now and Milo before Chad were not the same person."

Claire was looking forward to tremendous changes when it was time for Milo to go to public school in September with Chad at his side. One hurdle Claire had to clear was getting Milo's school to agree to let Chad accompany her son to classes every day. After much negotiation with the school, the school's attorneys, and Milo's doctor, the school said Chad could be with Milo one day per week only.

"This, of course, was completely unacceptable," says Claire. "I had to find a school that was willing to see outside the box and realize that having a child with a service dog was a huge benefit. Milo's doctor and therapist worked hard with me on this effort, and it finally paid off."

Today, Milo and Chad attend a private school called the Gersh Academy in Hauppauge, New York, on Long Island. They leave together on a bus at 7 A.M. and return home at 4 P.M.; in between, Milo is having the time of his life, Claire says. "The new school is wonderful, and the staff's attitude about having Chad with Milo has been inspiring. It's such a joy to see Milo come home from school happy every day. He never liked to go to school before, but all that has changed because of Chad."

One thing that made the transition to the new school so successful for Milo and Chad was the presence of Kati Rule-Witko, a trainer from the ASDA, who flew in from Oregon to help with in-school training. "The school staff spent some time working alone with Kati so they could help Milo acclimate better," Claire notes. "Kati said she was very impressed with the school, and because she visits every school where a dog from the Autism Service Dogs of America is placed, that comment meant a lot coming from her." (To learn more about Kati's work, see the story "Constant Companions," page 65).

Milo has begun to display self-confidence and self-esteem ever since Chad entered his life. "We can now do many more things that we couldn't do before," explains Claire. "Because Milo focuses on Chad, he is less likely to

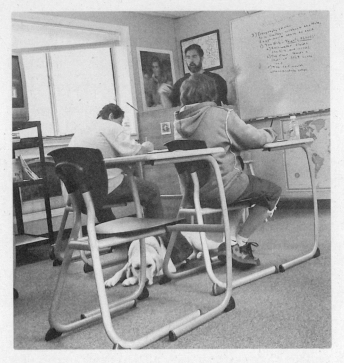

Milo and Chad at Milo's new school

focus on all the other sensory things in the environment that used to agitate or confuse him. Milo has become so expert at managing Chad on and off the city buses and subways that I see other people looking at him in amazement. Sometimes people will come up and ask him why he has a dog, and Milo can now confidently answer, 'This is my service dog for autism. I have autism.'"

Having Chad in their lives has been an education for Claire as well, who is now very fluent with the laws that are part of the Americans with Disabilities Act (ADA). "We've had to educate people who don't know about the ADA laws that allow Chad to go anywhere with Milo. The worst thing would be for Milo to feel limited by having Chad. We experienced a challenge at Milo's favorite Japanese restaurant, where they actually said right in front of Milo that 'he's not blind so he can't have his service dog in this restaurant.' We were able to eventually educate them about autism and now they are very welcoming of Milo and Chad, even to the point that we have a special table."

Claire is especially grateful that having Chad is making it possible for Milo to begin tapering off one of the very serious medications he has been on for several years. Although the drug was necessary for Milo to make the transition from hospital and residential living back to living at home with his family, having Chad has provided so much of a calming effect that Milo's doctor, Melissa Nishawala of the New York University Child Study Center, has approved decreasing this medication, which has irreversible side effects including tardive dyskinesia, a condition characterized by involuntary movements and vocal tics. Milo has also gained a significant amount of weight because of the drug, which has made him prediabetic. Getting Milo off this one medication could mean a great improvement in his health now and into the future.

Claire is still in awe of the changes in Milo. "He sings and dances and laughs every day. It's amazing," she says. "He is learning so much in school because his brain is calmer and he can digest information better. I know my son has much to offer the world. Chad will be his grounding body, to allow him to blossom and be the social and interesting boy I know he is."

The Rookie

Corrie Russinko

It was our first day on the "job." After we signed in at the hospital's volunteer office, we were instructed to go to the infusion center, where we would visit with patients who were receiving cancer treatments and dialysis.

My dog, Leilu, a red and white Border collie with one blue eye and one brown, is very true to her breed. She likes to work. I had been looking for some kind of outlet for her seemingly boundless energy. We had tried agility training, and although Leilu did well in the sport, I could tell that she wanted something more challenging, and so I signed up with The Good Dog Foundation for their ten-week training to become a therapy dog team.

Although I felt we had been well prepared by Good Dog, I think I can speak with some certainty when I say we were both a bit nervous that day. In the back of my mind, I had been wondering if all of the time and effort we had put into this project was going to be worth it. Today I would know.

Thankfully, the nurses were very welcoming and patient in guiding us around the hospital wing. As we approached the first patient, my eyes immediately went to the many tubes and wires surrounding her. But even before I was able to register any apprehension about how she might navigate all of this delicate equipment, I saw that Leilu was already carefully making her way to the woman's side. I will never forget the smile on this patient's face as Leilu approached.

We visited a few other patients and then I realized that we should begin to make our way out of the building, as it had been suggested at the volunteer center that we stay for only an hour or so. As we rode down together in the elevator, I felt a deep sense of satisfaction. While there had been nothing exceptionally noteworthy to report, we had had a good first day. Suddenly, in the lobby, I caught

Good Dog Leilu

sight of an obviously distressed older woman seated on a circular wooden bench near the exit door. A younger woman, who I assumed was her daughter, was sitting beside her, her arm around the older woman's shoulders. They were virtually motionless, their heads seeming to bow under an enormous weight of some kind. The wheels of my mind began to turn: What did we cover in our training classes that I could apply to this situation? Here were two more people who obviously needed help and support.

Leilu must have also sensed the gravity of the situation. Before I was able to make up my mind what—if anything—we should do, she'd decided for herself that she had one more visit to make before her work was done for the day. With great force, she pulled me over to the bench where they were sitting, sat down directly in front of the older woman, and immediately involved herself in the business of soliciting a pat. With a faint smile on her lips, the woman obliged and reached down to stroke Leilu's fur. After a few moments, I noticed that she had quietly begun to sob. I was totally taken aback to see Leilu look over her right shoulder and give me her "Can I, please, Mommy?" look, and I knew exactly what she wanted. She was asking for permission to get closer and to give this woman a hug.

I gave Leilu a nod that it was okay but I held on to her leash with extreme caution so I could lead her properly, just in case. My uneasiness quickly passed, however, as I watched my dog gently place her front paws, first one and then the other, on this woman's lap, and the two wrapped themselves in a tight embrace. Suddenly, the woman released her hold on Leilu as sobs issued from deep within. Leilu pulled away just enough to tenderly lick some of the tears off of her cheek. Eventually, they quietly returned to their hugging position.

At one point, the daughter and I glanced at each other and I saw that, like me, she had tears in her eyes. We held our gaze for a brief moment in recognition of what had just happened. It had been amazing to witness the healing power of this interaction between a dog and a human. After a few more minutes had passed, Leilu slowly backed down to a sit position and gave the two women one last chance to pet her head. I nodded a quick goodbye and we headed for the parking lot.

As I was driving home, I realized that not two words had been exchanged the whole time among the three of us. There was no conversation among us humans because, after all, what was there to say? Leilu took care of everything. She knew exactly what to do. Any questions I had had before about what we were doing and if it was going to be worthwhile, well, they were unequivocally answered that day.

Reading—Going to
the Dogs

I want to read this book again!" Jessica declared.

These are words that Carolyn never thought she would hear her seven-year-old daughter say, much less with so much enthusiasm. But Jessica isn't talking to her mother, or to her teacher, who is also in the room. Jessica is anxious to share her excitement about her book with Pepper.

Pepper is slightly overweight, has a tendency to cock his head to one side, and has one ear that stands up and one that flops over. When Jessica is reading, he is usually all ears, except when he dozes off, but Jessica doesn't mind. Pepper, an eight-year-old Border collie mix, is her friend.

"Pepper loves when I tell him stories," she says. "I think he likes stories about turtles best, and so do I. He's the coolest dog in the whole world."

Jessica and Pepper are part of The Good Dog Foundation Reading Program, which pairs dogs with children in an effort to improve reading skills and self-confidence as well as spark and foster in young children a lifelong interest in reading. In Jessica's case—and for hundreds of children in her school district and others in New York who are currently reading below grade level and experiencing other difficulties with reading—the effort is yielding impressive results.

The Good Dog Foundation Reading Program is in full swing in several schools in New York City and three branches of the New York Public Library system. Children in Spanish Harlem, in East Harlem, in the Bronx, and on the Upper West Side are among those who have an opportunity to participate in the program.

Barbara Christy, a third-grade teacher and the person in charge of this special reading club at her school, is setting up the classroom for the once-a-week reading group. The twelve children who participate in the program in this school are all struggling readers: In addition to reading below their grade level, they also have difficulty reading aloud and, consequently, they are having problems with other subjects and academic tasks. Their struggle with reading has had a global and devastating impact on their lives: They are often stigmatized by their peers and, not surprisingly, tend to lack confidence and have poor self-esteem.

But all that is changing—and it's all because of the dogs. "It's ironic," says Barbara. "The kids in the school can choose to participate in any one of many different clubs—sewing, cooking, arts and crafts, music—and yet many of them, who are good readers, want to stay with— to be associated with—the poor readers, the very same kids that they used to make fun of."

"Coming to the reading program is one of Jared's favorite things to do," says his mother, Charise, who has dropped by the classroom on her way home from work. "I think he may like it better than basketball." Jared scrunches up his face and looks at his mother. "Well, not better than basketball," he shoots back, and then slides easily into his campaign spiel. "If I had a dog at home, I could read at home. I could read lots and lots at home. If I had a dog like Marmaduke, I could do it."

Marmaduke is the five-year-old greyhound who hangs on Jared's every word as he reads from his favorite books. Today it's a book about space travel, and Jared says he wants to be an astronaut someday. And a basketball player. But first, says Charise, he must do well in school, and the reading program is helping him do just that.

"I've noticed a big improvement in his schoolwork," says Charise. "His teacher says he pays attention more in class. That's because now he's getting it; he can read better and he feels better about himself. And his behavior at home has improved as well. He's getting along with his brother and sister. He has more self-confidence, more of an 'I can do it' attitude. He reads aloud at home to me nearly every night, and I can hear the confidence in his voice. And he enjoys reading. I think this program has given him a chance to succeed."

While Charise has been talking, all three dogs— Abigail the standard poodle, Marmaduke the greyhound, and Pepper the Border collie—have each paired up with a child while the remaining children sit at desks and read aloud. They are waiting their turn with a dog, and Barbara circulates among the seated children and listens to each one to make sure they are truly reading and not pretending. The children know that they must keep reading aloud if they want a chance to read to a dog.

One of the children reading aloud at her desk is Malinda. "Just a few months ago, Malinda was the lowest reader in her third-grade class," says Barbara. Malinda often had stomachaches in the morning and had to be coaxed out the door. Once in school, she was terrified to read aloud, and her fear infiltrated every other part of her day. She barely talked to anyone, and her mother and teachers were about to refer her to the school psychologist. However, once she started working with a dog, the transformation was startling: Malinda blossomed, and the true, bright, more confident Malinda came out. Clearly the dog program has made a huge difference in her schoolwork and in her entire life.

Each child gets to spend about ten minutes with a dog, and then three more children replace the first three. None of the children fidget or waste time: They are eager to begin reading because they know their "dog time" is limited and

Good Dog Lily enjoying her favorite book

Good Dog Roxy

us. Some flop onto their stomach and read to the dog
.y nose to nose or cozy up immediately next to the
 g, hip to hip, on the rug. Others sit cross-legged next to
their canine pal. Each dog's owner is omnipresent, quietly
listening to the child read aloud and intervening only when
necessary to gently prompt the child if he or she has read a
word incorrectly or is struggling with a word.

Barbara says she is very impressed with the way the
children interact with the dogs' owners. "The children
are not intimated by the dogs' owners when they correct
or guide the children to reconsider a word they are struggling with," Barbara says. "It's as if the owners are not
viewed as adult authority figures but as an extension of
the dogs themselves. It's really quite amazing, and it
works so well."

Once all the children have had an opportunity to read
to a dog, Barbara and the children form a big circle. The
dogs and their owners settle in the center, where the dogs
perform tricks and the children can talk to the dogs and
ask questions. Then it's time for The Hugs, when each
child has a chance to enter the circle and hug the dog he
or she worked with.

"It's a 'three Mississippi' hug," says Barbara. "We
have to limit how long each child spends with the dog, or

the kids would want to hug the dogs all day long. The hugs are a way for the children to bond again with the dogs and to say good-bye until next week. For some of these children, this hug may be the only one they get all week. It's really a very emotional time."

It is hard to believe that in the not-so-distant past, these children were afraid to read aloud and often struggling with nearly every word. "Now they are loud and proud," Barbara points out. "Kids who used to slink into a room are walking tall, with their shoulders back and head up. One young man used to stutter; now his speech is nearly stutter-free. I tell everyone there's magic occurring every week in this classroom."

One of the most exciting spin-offs of the program is called Readers' Theater. The children choose a book and then each takes the part of one of the characters in the book and they present the story as a play. This idea has grown into a new venture proposed by the children: They want to write their own script about one of the reading dogs and its owner and present the play.

"Having the dogs as reading partners has triggered much more than better reading skills," Barbara notes. "These children are now motivated to write and perform. What terrific examples of self-confidence and creativity!"

27

When it's time for the circle to break up and for the reading club to end, no one wants to leave. Even the dogs seem to linger, as if they want yet another hug. They, like the children, want to hold on to the magic just a little bit longer.

Hooch

Just days after Christmas in 2004, Daniel Simone, a fiftyish, athletic, hardworking construction worker, was severely injured on the job when his leg was crushed by a crane. As part of an attempt to repair his leg, doctors put Daniel into an eight-day drug-induced coma. When Daniel was brought out of the coma, he discovered that he could not feel his newly rebuilt leg, and that despite their best efforts, the doctors believed the leg would need to be amputated in several years.

Daniel said, "Take it off now and let me get on with my life." So, in January 2005, Daniel said good-bye to his leg.

A leg wasn't the only thing that Daniel lost during this

trying time. While he was in a coma, his mother passed away. And whether or not you believe that bad news happens in threes, there was a third emotionally shattering event: Daniel's beloved Rottweiler had become very ill and was euthanized.

With three losses weighing heavily on Daniel, plus the fact that he was no longer able to work, he and his wife decided they needed a change of scenery, and so they moved from New York City to Tucson, Arizona. The desert environment did nothing to lift the depression and loneliness Daniel felt.

"I needed something to fill the void in my life," says Daniel. "And I knew that 'something' was another Rottweiler."

A trip to a small town just outside of Tombstone, Arizona, brought Daniel face-to-face with the Rottweiler that immediately stole his heart. Hooch was only ten weeks old when Daniel picked him out of a litter, and three weeks later the four-legged Rottie made the trip in his truck to his new home in Tucson.

As Daniel adjusted to his new life in the desert with his new artificial leg, his crutches, and his cane, he included Hooch in everything he did. Not one to sit still, Daniel began taking Hooch to the park every day. As dog

Daniel and Hooch

owners know, having a dog is one of the best conversation starters in the world, and Daniel and Hooch were no exception. One day a woman at the park with her dog told Daniel about Handi-Dogs, a service dog organization in Tucson. Handi-Dogs is different from many other service dog organizations in that it teaches people to work with their own dogs. Thus, people with disabilities, seniors who need assistance, and caregivers of people who need a service dog are all welcome to bring their dogs and go through the certification program.

Daniel was intrigued. He loved working with Hooch, and he felt the training would open up doors of opportunity for both of them. "With Hooch as my service dog, I realized I would have access to many more places, with no questions asked," says Daniel. "If I dropped my crutches or fell, Hooch would know how to help."

Daniel quickly discovered that the program was as much about training himself as it was about training Hooch. "The first year was torture," Daniel recalls. "Both of us weren't learning, and I was getting frustrated."

Then something clicked. A new trainer began working with them, and Daniel admits that "she pushed us hard. But once I was programmed, it was easy from then on." Two years after starting the beginner's class, Hooch passed his certification test the first time he took it. Now Hooch was a certified service dog.

But Daniel wanted more: He wanted to give back to the community, and to do that, Hooch also needed therapy dog certification. So Hooch completed the American Kennel Club's Canine Good Citizenship program, which is designed to reward dogs who have good manners at home and in the community. Daniel also enrolled Hooch in the Delta Society's Pet Partners Team Training program so they would be certified to visit nursing homes, classrooms, and other facilities. Hooch passed with flying colors.

Next stop, the Quincie Douglas Branch Library in southwest Tucson. When Hooch isn't wearing his service dog hat for Daniel, you might find him lying comfortably on the floor next to a child who is reading him a story. When Daniel first heard about the Reading Education Assistance Dogs (READ) program, which pairs dogs with children who need help with reading, he knew he wanted to get involved. See information about READ on page 226.

"I had trouble with reading as a kid, and I still don't read especially well," explains Daniel. "But I know how important it is, particularly in today's world. By participating in the READ program, it's a way for me to give back, to help kids have a better shot at life."

One child has especially captured the hearts of both Hooch and Daniel. When Daniel first brought Hooch to the library, there were many children who were excited about choosing a dog they could read to. Hooch, however, picked out who he wanted to partner up with, walking straight over to Carlos, a shy seven-year-old. Hooch encourages Carlos to read by nudging him when he stops, or he turns his huge head and looks at Carlos as if to say, "I can't hear you!"

"I can't tell you how thrilling it is to see Carlos and Hooch work together," says Daniel. "Hooch makes Carlos smile, and what could be better than making a child smile."

Ever looking for new challenges, Daniel has signed up himself and Hooch to be a team for Gabriel's Angels, an organization that sends handler-dog therapy teams to help children who have been abused or who have engaged in aggressive or criminal behaviors. "I've been there," says Daniel. "I was a delinquent as a teenager. I got arrested, spent some time in jail, and learned my lesson. I'd like to work with these kids and give them a chance."

In the meantime, Hooch continues to help Daniel live more independently. Weighing in at more than one hundred pounds, his size and brute strength come in especially handy, like when Daniel tripped and fell in the yard recently and hit his head. Hooch was there to help Daniel get up by allowing him to brace himself on the dog's back. When Daniel drops his crutches, Hooch is there to retrieve them.

"Getting Hooch to pick up the crutches actually took

some creative thinking," Daniel says. "It's hard to believe this huge dog is timid about anything, but Hooch doesn't like putting his mouth on metal. Because my crutches are metal, I wrapped them with pipe-insulating material so he would be comfortable picking them up."

It's early evening, and the desert is beginning to give up its heat. Hooch is ready for his nightly trip to the park, where he and Daniel will spend about an hour playing and socializing. "Hooch is much more than a service dog," Daniel observes. "He fills a void in my life. He gives unconditional love, he puts a smile on the faces of children. Like I said, what could be better than that?

Faith & Rocco

Peter Howe

First-time visitors to the Stephen D. Hassenfeld Children's Center for Cancer and Blood Disorders in midtown Manhattan are often surprised by its cheerful atmosphere. Given that it's a treatment center for children with life-threatening conditions, some of them as young as six months, it is surprisingly bright and lively. You enter past a huge tropical fish tank on your way to a playroom staffed with professionally trained art and occupational therapists; a game room is in constant use with mammoth contests of Wii basketball taking place; a fully stocked library caters to the needs of little book lovers; a clown does the rounds of the unit every day, making bad jokes and loud noises on an old-fashioned car horn. And then there is, of course, the pet therapy program, of which my dog, Rocco, a Samoyed, has been a key member since he graduated the youngest in his class at the age of ten months.

It was at Hassenfeld that Rocco and I met four-year-old Faith, who seemed to be an ideal candidate for pet therapy. She would be a long-term patient at the clinic, giving us ample time to encourage her to form a bond with my dog. Everything pointed to an extremely successful encounter of the kind that Rocco's Good Dog Foundation training prepared him for. There was only one problem—Faith was terrified of dogs.

R occo is the calmest dog I've ever known, almost preternaturally so. It was this quality that enabled Faith to overcome the fear she had that was the result of an unfortunate experience with a dog when she was very young. Faith had come to Hassenfeld from her home in Florida for three-month courses of treatment, and she was not alone. Her entire family moved into the Ronald McDonald House and stayed there for the duration— mother, father, and younger brother, plus a grandmother who came in from New Jersey. I've been doing this work for over thirteen years and I never cease to be amazed at the lengths that parents go to to protect and heal their children, and Faith's were up there in my pantheon of hero parents.

During our first few meetings, Faith's father or mother would bring her into the library where we work, and sit Faith down on his or her lap. Cautiously at first, I would bring Rocco near her, and over time closer and closer until finally she started to stroke him, groom him, and feed him treats. Not only did she soon come to trust Rocco, she became quite besotted with him. She would run into the library and throw her arms around him in an enormous hug. When Polaroid film was still available, I used to take "magic" pictures of clients with the dog for their keeping. In this digital age, most children have never seen a Polaroid picture "appear" before their eyes, and each week we would add another image to Faith's gallery. Her mother told me that when strangers came into their house in Florida for the first time, they would ask where the dog was because there were so many pictures of Rocco on display.

The most difficult part of working at Hassenfeld is

the fact that each year some of our clients don't make it, and little Faith was one of the unfortunate ones. Toward the end of her life, her disease robbed her of the ability to walk properly, and she had great difficulties with speech. Her father would still bring her into the library and sit her down on his lap. Without any prompting from me, Rocco would walk over to her, turn around the obligatory three times all dogs seem to need before lying down, and put his head in her lap. She would then stroke him, and they would remain like that for ten to fifteen minutes at a time. If you've never seen a child without the facility of speech silently relate with an animal, you've never really experienced the power of nonverbal communication that we've lost as we've become more complex beings. It is the most goose-bump-inducing situation I've ever known.

Faith was five when she died, and Rocco and I knew her for probably a total of nine months of her short life, but the memories I have of that little girl will remain with me for the rest of mine. She taught me that life goes on until it doesn't, and that the companionship of an animal is as valuable as any treatment that drips into your body through a tube.

Rocco and I now live in rural Connecticut, many miles from Hassenfeld, and every Tuesday when I drive into Manhattan and I'm stuck in traffic and surrounded by angry New York drivers, I wonder why I do this. Every Tuesday, as I leave the clinic, I have my answer.

Dog Medicine

Rachel McPherson and Grace A. Telesco

Rachel:

Despite the shock and sadness that I—along with the rest of the world—was experiencing in the wake of the horrible events of September 11, 2001, I knew almost immediately that the dogs we work with at The Good Dog Foundation had a great gift to share with the families of victims of this tragedy. In the week following 9/11, I spent a great deal of time trying to break through red tape to organize therapy dog visits. At week's end, we finally received permission for the dogs to participate in a program coordinated by the ASPCA at the New York City family assistance center at Pier 94 on Manhattan's West Side, which, in the days and weeks following the attack, offered services and crisis intervention for over 5,000 families who were affected.

I will never forget all of the people I spoke with that day and their grateful responses to the love and support offered to them by the dogs, but the look in one woman's eyes as my papillon, Fidel, walked up to her and gently placed his paws on her knee especially stays with me. She picked him up and held him in her arms, and almost immediately the tears began to flow. She looked up at me and asked, "How does this dog know that I am in such pain?" Many others would express the same awe at the power of the therapy dogs that day and in the months ahead.

During my visit at the center, I was honored to get to know Lieutenant Grace Telesco, the Inter-agency Coordinator for Mental Health Services at the Family Assistance Center. Grace came to me and asked if Fidel and I would be part of a mental health team that would go on the ferry each day to Ground Zero to visit the families of the victims. The first boat trip was held on September 22.

Good Dog Fidel

Grace:

In the days and weeks following the tragic events of September 11, various agencies and organizations became part of a unique support team. My unit in the New York City Police Department's Community Affairs Section was responsible for ensuring that the many services that were being offered to the families of victims—for example, the filing of missing-persons reports and the release of patient and deceased lists—were delivered safely and effectively. As a police lieutenant with a doctorate in the mental health field and extensive background in crisis intervention, I, along with a team of officers also chosen because of their expertise in crisis intervention, coordinated the interagency mental health response.

In Native American spirituality, the term "dog medicine" is used to describe the loyalty, service, and unconditional love that the greatest healers bestow upon their patients. The pet therapy provided by groups like the Delta Society, Therapet, Therapy Dogs International (TDI), and The Good Dog Foundation following 9/11 was an example of "dog medicine" at its very best. The therapy dogs I observed in the weeks after the attack instinctually understood where the families were emotionally. Without words, these dogs communicated—just with their very presence—a form of love, acceptance, and understanding that is hard to describe. Where a mental health practitioner's words, while well meaning, could not reach an individual, these dogs broke through barriers to forge deep connections with those who were suffering.

In response to the many pleas from family members

for access to Ground Zero, ferry rides were set up to take them to the site. The hope we all had was that this might help move these people toward some sense of closure. On one of these rides, an elderly Latina woman was so stricken with grief that she appeared inconsolable. Neither the officers from the mental health team, the Red Cross volunteers, nor the spiritual care providers were able to make a connection with her. On that trip was Fidel, a sweet, adorable, extraordinarily loving papillon, who was one of the most effective dogs I witnessed during this time. As this woman stood there holding Fidel in her arms while crying and sobbing uncontrollably, it was as if Fidel quite literally absorbed her grief. One of the most profound lessons I learned during those critical weeks following 9/11 was the importance of remaining nonintrusive and responding in a way that helped these individuals, who were at various stages in the mourning process, regain their dignity, power, and security. With his purely selfless support, Fidel was instrumental in helping this woman reach a catharsis, a first step in her recovery. After the trip, the woman thanked Fidel, who exhaustedly fell into a deep sleep in the arms of his owner, Rachel McPherson.

Fidel and the many other dogs who were there for us humans during this dark time gave *all* of us—including us caregivers, who greatly needed the dogs' support in order to be strong for the victims—one of the greatest gifts you can give to another being: the gift of unconditional love.

Closing Tails

Dogs As Healers and Teachers

This section contains stories about dogs that help people who have a variety of physical, educational, or emotional needs. Perhaps these tales have piqued your interest in working with your dog to help others, or perhaps you just want to know more about dogs that teach and heal. If so, there are two things you can do.

One, you can read the rest of this section, where we talk about service dogs. Dogs that help humans are often referred to as therapy dogs or service dogs, and the terms are frequently used interchangeably, but they should not be, as they are two distinctly different types of specially trained canines. Dogs that assist people who have a disability are *service* dogs, and we discuss them below.

Two, if you are interested in becoming a volunteer with your dog so you can visit patients in hospitals, read to children, comfort the sick and lonely, and provide similar services, these are things *therapy* dogs do. To find out more, you can turn to section four, "Getting Involved: How to Become a Handler-Dog Therapy Team," where you can learn in detail what it takes to be part of a handler-dog therapy team.

Service Dogs

The Americans with Disabilities Act defines "service dog" as any guide dog, signal dog, or other animal who is trained to provide assistance to an individual with a disability. For example, some dogs are trained to pull wheelchairs; others are taught to alert their owners to the sounds of the telephone, oven timers, alarm clocks, smoke alarms, and even a baby's cry. Service dogs are not considered pets.

Unlike therapy dogs, service dogs and their human companions must be allowed access to buildings (includ-

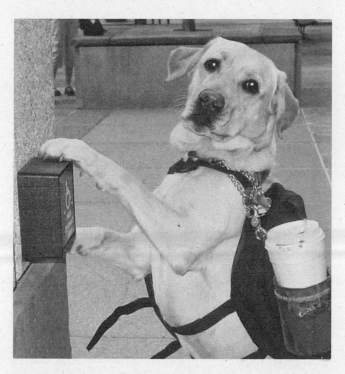

Pax, formerly a homeless-shelter dog, is now a Freedom Service Dog. Freedom Service Dogs help individuals with physical and/or emotional disabilities live their lives more independently.

Autism Service Dogs
of America

A lthough the concept of service dogs for people living with autism is relatively new, the awareness of and demand for such dogs are growing exponentially.

Autism Service Dogs of America (ASDA) trains specialized service dogs specifically for the purposes of assisting children living with the complicated and challenging conditions of autism. All of these unique dogs go through a rigorous training process, and are then carefully integrated into their new families. Since these very special service dogs are not serving a person with an overt sensory or physical disability (i.e., the dog is not leading a deaf or a blind person), they are sometimes mistaken for therapy dogs. But these dogs attend to their masters in a service dog capacity, accompanying them wherever they go, including restaurants, movie theaters, and even school. The benefits that these dogs provide to their families

Milo's dog, Chad ("A Gift for Milo"), was one of a litter of four dogs trained by Autism Service Dogs of America. From left to right: Chester, Chewey, Chad, and Chloe.

are absolutely remarkable, as evidenced by Claire Vaccaro's story, "A Gift for Milo" (see page 3) and ASDA trainer Kati Rule-Witko's story, "Consant Companions" (see page 65).

To find out more information about ASDA, view frequently asked questions, begin the application process, or donate to this groundbreaking organization, please visit their website at www.autismservicedogsofamerica.org.

ing restaurants, libraries, supermarkets, and churches), transportation systems, and other public areas and services. Another difference between therapy and service dogs is that the latter are often picked by breed for certain characteristics.

What It Takes to Be a Service Dog

Service dogs should have all the characteristics of a therapy dog, plus a few others. For example, certain breeds are chosen for specific types of service. In the United States, 60 to 70 percent of all working guide dogs for the blind are Labrador retrievers. Golden retrievers and German shepherds are next in popularity. These dogs are chosen because of their temperament, versatility, size, intelligence, and availability. Guide dogs must be hard workers, large enough to guide people while in harness and small enough to be easily controlled, and fit comfortably on public transportation and under restaurant tables.

You may find that some service dogs seem to "push the envelope" when it comes to fitting comfortably in public places. One such dog appears in this volume in section one. Hooch is a massive Rottweiler who is a service dog for Daniel. Although Hooch weighs in at more than one hundred pounds, he manages to wrap himself around the pedestal of a café table and be as unobtrusive as possible!

Raising a Service Dog Puppy

No dog is born a service dog: He or she needs to be trained and nurtured. That process begins, quite naturally, when the dog is a puppy, and it requires a dedicated individual.

One very important way people can volunteer to help service dog organizations is to become volunteer puppy raisers of future service dogs. Generally puppy raisers receive puppies that are around eight weeks of age and commit to keep and care for them for the next fourteen to eighteen months, depending on the program. The task of puppy raisers is to provide a safe, loving environment for the dogs, to take them to the scheduled obedience classes arranged by the sponsoring organizations, and to expose them to lots of opportunities for socialization. Typically they must also regularly submit reports on the dogs' progress as well.

Volunteer puppy raisers are needed by service dog

Gus is being trained by Autism Service Dogs of America to become a service dog. To find out more about puppy-raising volunteer opportunities, visit www.austismservice dogsofamerica.org.

organizations that serve the blind, the hearing impaired, the physically disabled, children with autism, and people with other disabilities. It is important to note that puppy raisers do *not* train the puppies to be service dogs; they provide the critical foundation of socialization, love, and obedience necessary for the dogs to become effective service dogs. Well-socialized puppies have fewer adjustments to make when it comes time for them to enter formal guide dog or service dog training. Without dedicated puppy raisers, service dog organizations would not be able to provide service animals to people in need.

Below we briefly explain the puppy-raising programs for two organizations, Guide Dogs of America and Fidelco, so you can get an idea of what being a volunteer puppy raiser involves. There are dozens of organizations that need these special services from volunteers. We have included a list of a few of them at the end of this section.

GUIDE DOGS OF AMERICA

Volunteer puppy raisers for Guide Dogs of America must first complete an application and be interviewed before a puppy is placed in their care. (Puppy raisers must live in southern or central California; some parts of Washington also participate.) At the interview, puppy raisers are given a thirty-page manual that explains their tasks. When a puppy is assigned to a volunteer, the puppy raiser also receives a bowl, brush, bone, leash, collar, ID tag, puppy jacket, and ID card.

Food and any other items that volunteers purchase

for the dog are tax deductible. Guide Dogs of America pays all veterinary bills.

Puppy raisers are required to teach the puppies basic obedience, such as how to sit, lie down, walk properly on a leash, and come when called, all through an approved obedience class. They also must attend monthly meetings, which serve as socialization events for the puppies and the volunteers, who can compare notes and stories with one another.

A critical part of puppy raising is socialization. Puppies wear a puppy jacket whenever they are out in public, and as future service dogs they have the same rights and privileges as service dogs. (Note: This right is not granted by every state. The organization you work with will let you know the laws in your state.) That means they have access to public places such as malls, movie theaters, restaurants, grocery stores, and so on.

When puppies are about eighteen months old, it is time for volunteers to turn them over to the organization for formal guide dog training. Guide Dogs of America holds a Barbecue for Puppy Raisers so all the volunteers and their puppies can get together for one last time. Formal guide dog training takes about four to six months.

Puppy raisers are not allowed to visit with their puppy during that time, but once training is done, they can go to the Awards Ceremony and meet the individuals who will receive the dogs they raised.

FIDELCO GUIDE DOG FOUNDATION

Fidelco, based in Bloomfield, Connecticut, utilizes their own stock of German shepherd dogs bred for intelligence, temperament, stamina, and stability.

The volunteer, or "foster," begins their puppy foster program with an eight-week-old puppy. The foster and his or her puppy spend time on housebreaking, basic obedience, car rides, frequent walks, and trips to public places. The pup is exercised on a lead and is always supervised.

Puppy fosters participate in weekly socialization and training exercises at the Fidelco training center and then, when the pups are around fourteen to sixteen months old, return them for their six- to nine-month formal guide dog training. Once the dogs are placed with Fidelco clients, the fosters are given photos of the dogs wearing guide dog harnesses. They are also invited to participate in a graduation walk.

Resources

American Dog Trainers Network

www.tonypassera.com/thedogsite/www/new/

This website lists service dog resources throughout the United States by state.

Angel on a Leash

www.angelonaleash.org

Provides customized therapy dog programs to facilities across the country.

Bunny Bud Books

www.bunnybudbooks.com

This is the publisher of *The Rainbow Series: Dogs Who Help,* an ongoing series of nonfiction children's books about real dogs who help people in different ways. The books are geared toward children from preschool through fifth grade. Each book has at least one life "lesson" about animal stewardship, acceptance, and diversity.

Canine Companions for Independence

www.cci.org/site/c.cdKGIRNqEmG/b.3978475/k.BED8/ Home.htm

This organization has provided highly trained assistance dogs for people with disabilities since 1975. It is a nationwide organization with many regional offices.

"Children's Disabilities Information"

www.childrensdisabilities.info/therapy-service-animals/ therapy-dog-special-education.html

An article on dog therapy in special education classrooms.

Delta Society

www.deltasociety.org/Page.aspx?pid=183

An organization dedicated to improving human health through the use of service and therapy animals.

Dogs for the Deaf

www.dogsforthedeaf.org

A nonprofit organization that rescues homeless dogs from

shelters in California, Oregon, and Washington and professionally trains them to help the deaf.

Fidelco Guide Dog Foundation

www.fidelco.org

A nonprofit organization that breeds, trains, and places German shepherd guide dogs throughout North America.

The Good Dog Foundation

www.thegooddogfoundation.com

Guide Dogs for the Blind

www.guidedogs.com

A guide dog training school that offers guide dogs and training free of charge to blind and visually impaired people throughout the United States and Canada.

Handi-Dogs, Inc.

www.handi-dogs.org

An organization dedicated to enhancing the quality of life of seniors and people with disabilities by teaching them to train their own dogs to become assistance (service) dogs.

Hearing Loss Web

www.hearinglossweb.com/res/dog/dog.htm

A website that provides access to many articles on hearing dogs.

Intermountain Therapy Animals

www.therapyanimals.org

Specializes in providing animal assistance in physical therapy, occupational therapy, speech therapy, and psychotherapy, as well as special education.

Puppies Behind Bars

www.puppiesbehindbars.com

An organization that trains inmates to raise puppies to become service dogs for the disabled and explosive detection canines for law enforcement.

BOOKS

Burch, Mary B., Ph.D. *Volunteering with Your Pet: How to Get Involved in Animal-Assisted Therapy with Any Kind of Pet.* **New York: Howell Book House, 1996.**

An overview of animal-assisted therapy and how to get started.

EVERY DOG HAS A GIFT

Hoffman, Martha. *Lend Me an Ear: The Temperament, Selection and Training of the Hearing Ear Dog.* Wilsonville, OR: Doral Publishing, 1999.

Contains tips, trainers' secrets, and information about this fast-growing facet of the assistance dog industry.

Presnall, Judith. *Animals with Jobs: Hearing Dogs.* Detroit: Thomson Gale, 2004.

A book for children ages nine through twelve. Explains how hearing dogs alert their deaf or hearing-impaired masters to ordinary household noises such as alarm clocks, telephones, oven timers, and smoke alarms.

2

dogs that
change lives

Constant Companions

Kati Rule-Witko has always had a passion for dogs. One of those little girls who loved to spend hours "training" her dogs to do various tricks, dogs have always been an important part of her life. But around the age of twelve, a new passion began to take hold: helping kids with disabilities. Kati's mom runs a preschool in Oregon where she grew up. At any given time, there were a few kids with disabilities attending the school. Kati spent a lot of time helping her mom provide a warm and nurturing environment in which they could grow and develop. Her two interests coincided for some years, but it wasn't until she started doing

Kati, Chewey, and Kaleb (from left) preparing
for a training session

research for a senior project in college that they began to
fuse in a very exciting way.

Kati has an undergraduate degree in psychology and
special education with a focus on autism. During all four
years of college, Kati worked at a "group home" that
housed five children with autism. These were kids who—
for various reasons—could not live with their parents
and needed twenty-four-hour care. One day, Kati decided to bring her Labrador, Duke, to work with her, and
the response from the kids was amazing. "Duke had this

way of motivating the kids to do things they were fearful or uncomfortable about doing. For example, one boy had a problem with personal hygiene—he hated taking a shower. But if Duke would lie on the floor in the bathroom beside the tub, he'd do it." Kati was inspired to find out more about how this gift that dogs had for helping kids with autism worked and if it could be expanded upon in some way to help more children and families living with autism. As luck would have it, Kati found her way to a new organization recently founded in Oregon that was doing cutting-edge work with exactly this aim in mind.

For the past four and half years, Kati has been working with Autism Service Dogs of America and its founder and director Priscilla Taylor to train dogs to provide vital assistance to the now one-in-one-hundred kids diagnosed with autism each year. Says Kati, "This incredibly special thing happens when these dogs and these kids form partnerships. Children with autism need predictability and the dogs become this predictable thing in their life that never leaves their side. They both know that the dog is there to help them stay calm. I am fascinated by this understanding that they have about each other."

Once the two-year training process is completed and

a dog has been living with his new family for a few weeks, Kati travels to the family's home to facilitate the necessary training and to help the child and dog acclimate to the child's school and other settings in which they will now exist as a pair. She says that quite frequently when she arrives, she is astonished at how quickly the benefits of the partnership between dog and child can be seen. She tells a story about a seven-year-old boy in California whose mom told Kati that it was a herculean effort to physically get her son into the school building each day. And when it was time for her to leave him, he would engage in self-injurious behaviors, such as banging his head on the floor. On the very first day that their new service dog, Lily, accompanied the little boy to school, Kati remembers feeling anxious about what might occur. As it turned out, the little boy just strode right into the building and walked independently down the hall to his classroom, reaching down every so often to stroke Lily's fur. His teacher said it was the first time that he did not become upset or hurt himself following his mom's departure. She told them that after Kati and the boy's mother left, he curled up on the floor next to Lily and began to gently nudge his head against her furry stomach.

It's not all work and no play for the dogs though. Kati

says that part of the training involves instilling an under-standing in the dogs that when their packs are on, they are on duty, and when their packs comes off, they are regular old dogs. "It's important for them to get to be dogs because it's the dogness in them that makes them able to work so effectively with the children. The emo-tional component is essential—dogs work to earn our love, it's what motivates them. And this doesn't just go one way. The kids also need their dogs to be friends, not just workers."

So many kids around the world beg their parents for a dog to love and these kids have this wish fulfilled, and so much more: They get their freedom in a world in which it is often challenging for their parents to keep them safe. On another "first day on the ground," Kati had been briefed by a mom in Florida that there was a certain spot along the path that she and her son always took when they walked into town that they just couldn't get past without her son screaming and attempting to bolt away from her. When feeling overstimulated or upset, many children with autism attempt to run. This mother knew this but just couldn't figure out what was triggering it or how to stop it. And so, each time they neared this spot, she held on tightly to her child, fearing

Kati and ASDA volunteer Kelly Sosa (on right) with
yellow lab Chester, black shepherd mix Dannie and,
standing on Kati is Dixie.

what might happen if he slipped loose and ran into the
road. Kati was there to help the service dog—a strong,
handsome yellow Lab named Comet—help the mother
and son navigate this challenge. She felt the full weight
of this mother's stress and anxiety and hoped that she
and Comet could help them.

They started their walk with the little boy holding on
tightly to Comet's handle. The mom said, "Okay, here
comes the spot." And to their surprise the little boy just
continued to march along calmly with the dog. A collec-

tive sigh of relief could be felt as the four continued on. Suddenly, Kati eyed a small water fountain that had been beautifully handcrafted with shining tiles standing in front of the post office on the other side of the street. Children with autism are frequently attracted to things that shimmer. She pointed it out to the mother and the realization hit them both at once: Consumed by the fear that she could not protect her child, the mother had not noticed that all he wanted was to touch and drink from this glittering fountain. The four crossed the street to enjoy the spectacle of the fountain close up and the joy on the child's face was palpable. The mom expressed to Kati what a great relief it would now be to know that she would not be so alone, that there would now be someone there to help her and her son to not only navigate the world more safely but to enjoy it more as well: They had Comet.

"When I first started doing this work, I was so excited about how much dogs can help these kids," Kati says, "but lately I am seeing more and more what a huge impact they can have on the whole family. For many of the families we work with, it's like they are finally able to really become a part of their communities again. They are able to do activities like going out to dinner or going to the grocery store as a family without fearing that they will have to explain why their child is having a meltdown because the meltdowns don't happen as often, or they don't last as long."

Kati also explains that the dogs help to prevent and ultimately decrease these meltdowns by being a constant in the child's life. And beyond the assurance that their presence provides, they are also specifically trained to give the children the help they and their families need. For example, because the child is now able to walk alongside their dog instead of walking with their parent grasping on to their shirt or arm, they have more independence and freedom. The dogs are also trained to nudge with their nose or kiss the child when he or she is distressed, thereby redirecting the child out of this state. Many kids with autism also need deep pressure to alleviate anxiety, and the dogs are trained to supply this deep pressure to the child's back or body.

Kati and ASDA are helping hundreds of children around the world and their families lead happier, more normal lives, and the work is incredibly satisfying. But there is one question she is asked frequently: How can you bear to say good-bye to these dogs who you become so close to during the two-year training process? "It's

On the first day of training for these eight-week-old ASDA puppies, Kati teaches them how to band together behind her and also how to walk with packs on!

hard to say good-bye. It's sad but it's like sending your kid off to college. You're proud. You know that it's now time for them to go out into the world and make their mark." In the case of the ASDA dogs, that mark will definitely be a lasting one.

Starting Over

Alison was giving a talk to a group of six- to eight-year-old children at a homeless shelter with her guide dog, Winnie, by her side. She talked about what it was like to be blind and let a dog be your eyes.

"Winnie gives me independence. Do you know what that means?" Alison asked. A few seconds of silence passed before a small voice from the back of the group said, "It means you are free."

When Alison became blind in 1994, the vivacious, optimistic, and outgoing young woman—who had been married for a mere six months, who had a career with the

Central Intelligence Agency, and who loved skiing and other outdoor sports—had to relearn her world and redefine her life. To increase her challenge, the diabetes she suffered from had taken its toll on her kidneys and pancreas, and her doctors told her that she needed to undergo double-kidney and pancreas transplants.

Alison needed a guide dog and reached out to Guiding Eyes for the Blind, but the surgery came first, and in December 1995 she underwent the procedure successfully.

To qualify for a guide dog, Alison had to complete two training programs. The first course taught her how to maintain her home, perform daily activities, and walk with a cane. When her "blind" rehabilitation was complete in January 1997, she was accepted into a training program to prepare her for receiving her guide dog.

Alison entered a class with eleven other students, all of whom were eager to find the best dog to fit their needs. Once the instructors evaluated Alison's abilities, they matched her with Colleen, a yellow Lab that was to become her first set of eyes. The training was hard, but Alison felt an ever-increasing sense of confidence as she worked with Colleen. When they had to go out into the community alone, complete a specific route, and return to the training facility as part of their final "exam," she and Colleen finished without a hitch. Alison said that for the first time since she lost her sight, she felt independent and confident.

After the graduation ceremony, Alison went home and took stock of her life. She felt good. She was only thirty-six, and with Colleen at her side she felt she could take on the world. Rather than return to her old job at the CIA, she decided to enroll in college and get her master's degree. Colleen made it possible for Alison to take the bus to college and go to all of her classes. She finished her communications degree with a specialty in public relations, and as she and Colleen walked up to the stage to accept the diploma, the dean announced that the dog deserved one as well for having attended all of Alison's classes!

It wasn't long before Alison was being asked by community groups, schools, businesses, and churches to give presentations on how it felt to work with a guide dog. Clearly there was a demand for her story. So, armed with a determination to succeed and a master's degree in communications, she launched her own business giving motivational talks. She also eagerly agreed to speak on behalf of Guiding Eyes for the Blind whenever asked, which she felt was her way of giving back for the gift of sight she had received.

In 2004, as Alison's enthusiasm and energy soared, Colleen's concentration levels began to wane. Alison knew it was time to make the decision to retire Colleen, because a guide dog that cannot focus is a danger to her partner. Colleen remained with Alison as a much loved pet for the rest of her life, but a black Lab named Winnie took over Colleen's job as guide dog.

While Colleen had been reserved and confident, Winnie was an extrovert—frisky, athletic, and eager to please. Together, Alison and Winnie became a more adventurous and physically active team. Alison had always loved horses, and when she learned that her autistic nephew was involved in equine therapy, she was eager to learn more and arranged to accompany him to the training facility.

There, Alison met the boy's instructor, and it wasn't long before she convinced Alison to return to the saddle— not only for her own pleasure, but to become a riding instructor to work with children who had physical or mental challenges. Alison did not need much convincing, as Winnie seemed more than ready for the new experience as well. So, with the help of several riding instructors and Winnie, of course, who quickly learned how to work with

Alison and Winnie

horses, Alison completed the requirements to be a certified therapeutic riding instructor, becoming the first person with any type of disability to receive this certification
in the United States.

Around that time, Alison struck up a friendship with
a quadriplegic man named Russell while they were both

lobbying in Washington for the rights of the disabled. He was an avid sailor, which Alison had been before losing her sight.

One day Russell phoned and said that he was short a crew member for his racing sloop. Was Alison interested?

Unlikely as it sounds, Alison did not hesitate: Perhaps her work with horses had boosted her confidence to take on more physical challenges. She went to Newport, Rhode Island, and Russell showed her what to do. Because he had mobility in his shoulders, he could be secured to the steering wheel of the boat and steer by moving his shoulders. He was Alison's eyes, and she was his arms and legs, able to move about the boat and handle the ropes and sails. Winnie was there, of course, and took to the new challenge with relish. Soon he was climbing the ladder in and out of the cabin below and wearing his own life vest.

As if having a blind woman and a quadriplegic man navigate a sailboat for leisure weren't a big enough challenge, Russell and Alison tried and then qualified for the North American Challenge Cup Regatta, a sailboat race in which all the participants are physically challenged. Russell and Alison traveled to Chicago in August 2008 for the paralympic event, and although they did not win, the experience left Alison with an even stronger hunger to sail.

Alison's husband also had sailing fever, and when an opportunity arose to renovate an old sailboat, he and Alison jumped at the chance. Once the boat was waterworthy, they named her *Colleen*, in honor of Alison's first guide dog, who had died at age twelve and a half. Today, when Alison isn't doing public speaking or running Alison's Whispers, her therapeutic riding program for challenged youngsters, you might find her with her husband and Winnie out on *Colleen*, looking for new experiences just over the horizon.

Dogs of Freedom

The secret of happiness is freedom.
The secret of freedom is courage.

—THUCYDIDES (460–404 BC)

In Denver, Colorado, Freedom Service Dogs rescues dogs to free people—individuals who have physical and/or emotional disabilities—so they can live their lives more fully. Freedom Service Dogs also frees dogs— saving them from an uncertain future—because its mission is to rescue abandoned, unwanted dogs for service dog training. Part of the mission includes training at-risk youth and women prisoners to train dogs for Freedom Service Dogs.

Artie Guerrero knows something about fighting for freedom on several fronts. A Vietnam veteran, he was wounded four times in the war. But the wounds to both his shoulders, his left leg, and his right hand were not the sole reason he has needed braces on both legs since 1967. Artie also has multiple sclerosis (MS), a degenerative disease that has left him wheelchair-bound since 1987.

But none of these physical limitations has stopped Artie from fighting for other freedoms here on the home front—veterans' rights—although the task has always been difficult to do from a wheelchair. Now in his sixties, Artie has been advocating for his fellow soldiers for nearly forty years by speaking in Washington, D.C., and at Veterans Administration hospitals and facilities around the country.

Until early 2009, Artie had been doing battle on his own. That's when Sierra, a three-year-old Lab that graduated from Freedom Service Dogs, became Artie's service dog and companion.

"Sierra has made a total difference in my whole attitude toward life," Artie says. "A doctor once asked me, 'Do you have MS or does MS have you?' Sierra has definitely helped me avoid having MS take over me. She allows me to be independent. My blood pressure has improved considerably since Sierra came into my life. But most of all she is my companion and best friend."

Sierra is actually the first dog to be placed as part of a new program under the auspices of Freedom Service Dogs. Called Operation Freedom, the program focuses specifically on placing service dogs with veterans who have special needs. Artie is the first recipient—and the head cheerleader, although he is too humble to accept the title—of this new venture, which is actively seeking veterans to match with dogs that are coming into the program.

At first, Artie wasn't sure he was the right person for the job of bringing together disabled vets with service dogs. Although he had been lobbying for veterans' rights for decades, he says he learned a thing or two: "One, it's difficult to get veterans to do things unless they see other vets do it first. They want to see that it works." Also, Artie was used to devoting his efforts to large groups of people who needed assistance. If he were to accept this challenge, he would be matching a dog with a vet, and that required an individual vet to openly acknowledge that he or she needed help.

Artie became convinced that he should take on the job when he saw how the trainers worked with the dogs and the meticulous care that went into fine-tuning their skills to meet the needs of disabled people. He knew he

Artie and Sierra

was witnessing a truly remarkable process, so he went through the training with Sierra. Artie believes veterans will appreciate the dedication, training, and courage it takes to become and to work with a therapy dog. He just needs to get that message across to veterans. Sierra makes it easier for him to do that.

"Sierra has a way of stealing the show," says Artie. "No matter where we go to talk about Operation Freedom—veterans' groups, VA hospitals, officials at the Veterans Administration—Sierra is the star. I tell everyone at the presentation that Sierra is with me wherever I go. Sierra demonstrates some of her skills, like picking up keys from the floor, opening doors, retrieving papers. I explain that at home and out in the community she does other tasks, such as taking laundry out of the washer, picking up my mail, and opening handicapped doors. I pass out brochures about Freedom Service Dogs and Operation Freedom to the vets and offer to give them more information if they want it. No hard sell, no pressure."

Artie saves some of his hard sell for another audience: the at-risk youth that help train dogs for Freedom Service Dogs as part of a program called Positive Connections. Both Sierra and Artie visit with these kids and emphasize how important their work is in teaching commands to future service dogs.

"It's a win-win," says Artie. "The kids gain a sense of purpose and self-esteem by making this important contribution in educating the dogs so they can be placed with vets. For most of these kids, participating in this program is the only positive validation they've ever had in their lives."

Another potential win-win situation is in the pipeline for Operation Freedom: a program in which veterans who have posttraumatic stress disorder (PTSD) learn to train the dogs, who will then be placed with physically disabled vets. For the vets with PTSD, the experience of working with the dogs can give them a sense of purpose and have a stabilizing effect on their lives. "Vets helping vets, dogs helping vets, vets helping dogs," Artie observes. "It's a complete circle."

Artie hopes to get that circle moving soon. Recently he was at the hospital pharmacy with Sierra, and two vets with PTSD were standing around waiting for their medication. They got curious about Sierra and started asking questions. This is the kind of interaction that Artie and Sierra like: relaxed, no pressure, where vets can get a good picture of what a service dog can do (Sierra just *has* to do a few tricks!) without making a commitment. But the seed is planted. And that's what Artie and Sierra want to keep doing: planting seeds of hope and healing.

For Artie, the healing is not over. Recently he had surgery to replace his right shoulder, which took a bullet from an AK-47 in Vietnam in 1967. Sierra visited him at the hospital, and since his return home she has not left his side. "I now believe there is some special healing power in Sierra and other service dogs," Artie says. "I can't explain it, but I know it's there—there for me and for others with special needs too."

Home Is Where
the Dog Is

Deborah Mitchell

I don't know how Pixel came to enter Dave's life. All I know is that the bond between this Benji-look-alike and his forty-something homeless companion was truly beautiful. Pixel and Dave were a completely unconventional family, but a family nonetheless.

I do remember how Pixel entered my life: It was about 7 A.M. on a Sunday morning as I was on my way to volunteer at a homeless shelter. I stopped to buy gas and had to go into the convenience store to pay the clerk when I saw a small dog sitting outside the front door. There was one other person in front of me at the register, and after he paid and left the building, I paid for my gas and did the same. Yet, when I got outside, I noticed that the dog was still sitting there and that the parking lot was empty. Either the person who had just left had forgotten his dog, or this dog had been abandoned earlier. I went back into the store and asked the clerk if she had noticed anyone with the dog and how long the dog had been there.

"The dog wasn't there when I started my shift at 5 A.M.," she said, "but I guess he's been sitting there about an hour. I never saw anyone with the dog."

The dog had a collar, but the tag on it said CALIFORNIA 1999 and this was Arizona in 2002, so it looked like whoever had left this dog didn't care enough to keep the license up to date. I pulled my car up to the front of the store, opened the passenger-side door, and the dog hopped in with little encouragement. *Great*, I thought, *perhaps she's friendly enough to take to the homeless shelter.*

The dog proved to be a huge success at the shelter, where I was able to put her in an enclosure with shade and water while I helped sort and pack clothes and toiletries for the homeless clients. Many of the homeless men stopped to talk to her, and the dog seemed to love the attention. While at the homeless facility, I reported the lost dog and left my number at the local animal shelter and the Humane Society, but I didn't expect a reply. After several hours of touring the unit with the dog, for whom I was already formulating a name, I headed for a picnic with friends, where again the dog made friends quickly. Sierra? Cheyenne? Montana? A flood of names went through my mind as I drove home with the dog.

The call on my answering machine took me by surprise. The message had been left about two hours earlier: The caller said he was at a pay phone and would be waiting by the phone until I called back. The voice was shaky, and I couldn't decide if the man was drunk or crying or perhaps both. He said he normally sold newspapers on the median of the highway and that the newspaper dispatcher had switched his sales spot that morning, which was why he had gotten separated from his dog. Would I please, please call him?

I hesitated. I had already bonded with the dog, but I knew I had to place this call. When I did, the man, who said his name was Dave, was clearly drunk, but even through the slurred speech I could detect his real affection for the dog, whose name was Pixel.

"I can prove she's my dog," he said. "Tell her to give

you a high-five and hold up your hand." I did, and the dog lifted her paw. I knew then that any hope I had of keeping this dog was gone, and I assured Dave I would deliver Pixel to him right away at the convenience store parking lot.

Twenty minutes later, Dave and his dog were reunited. Tears were streaming down his face as Pixel leapt from the car. Dave was in clean, well-worn jeans and a T-shirt with a cigarette pack rolled up in the sleeve. He was missing most of his front teeth, which made his smile seem even bigger than it was.

"I don't have much, but let me give you something for your trouble," he said. I told him that wasn't necessary, that it had been my pleasure to reunite him with his dog. Then I found myself telling him about Pixel's time at the homeless shelter and how she had put a smile on the face of the men who dropped by.

"You're a real nice lady," Dave said. "You can come and visit Pixel anytime you want. And you can bring Pixel to the shelter anytime you want. Just come to my corner and let me know."

Thus began a two-year friendship with a man and his dog, who was his owner's only family. Dave and Pixel lived alongside a dry riverbed behind a big-box store not far from where he sold newspapers. He had a tent, a fire pit, and a few lawn chairs salvaged from various dumps so he and his friends could sit around. But most of the time Dave spent time away from his camp, out on the median selling newspapers or walking around the northwest side of Tucson, with Pixel at his side.

Pixel did not want for food or clothing, as Dave's regular customers showered her with dog treats, dog food, and cash, especially around Christmastime. I, too, brought food to Dave from time to time, and whenever he had finished selling his newspapers for the day, he would sit and talk with me, telling me how he had been out on the streets for about twenty years, ever since he was discharged from the army during the Vietnam War, and how Pixel had made such a huge difference in his life.

"Until I got Pixel, I didn't trust anybody or anything," Dave said. "I found her about four years ago, wandering the streets of Las Vegas after dark. I was lonely, and so was she. We've been together ever since."

Dave came to trust me, and I became a surrogate "sister" to this drifter and his dog. He carried around my name and phone number in his pocket as the person to contact in case of emergency, and he said that if anything ever happened to him, he wanted me to have Pixel and take care of her. I said that I would.

When the brutal heat of Tucson summers came around, Dave and Pixel would hitch a ride with any trucker who was headed to Montana or Wisconsin, looking for work wherever Dave could find it, then head back down to Tucson in September. Shortly after the second summer that I knew them, Dave and Pixel returned to Tucson and within days I got a call from Dave, telling me that he had been in a fight and needed to hide out for a while. He told me where he and Pixel would be staying, and I went down to meet them. That's when he told me that he needed to get out of town, that the man he had beat up had pressed charges, and that the police were looking for him. Would I take him to Phoenix?

Before dawn on a Friday morning, I picked up Dave and Pixel and we drove to Phoenix, where I happened to have other business. I dropped them off in a parking lot, gave them a little cash and some dog treats, and hugged them both good-bye. Dave said they would come back in a few months, after things had cooled down. The guy who had pressed charges was a drifter, too, and Dave figured he would soon be heading out of town as well.

About three months later I saw one of Dave's friends, Tony, and asked him if he had heard anything about Dave and Pixel and when they would be coming back.

"Heard just a few days ago that Dave got picked up in Texas and was thrown in jail," said Tony. "Heard they took his dog away from him, too."

I needed details: Where in Texas? What was he arrested for? Where was Pixel? Why hadn't anyone called me? Dave always carried my name and number with him. Tony couldn't provide any more information, saying that it was just something he had heard from a guy who was passing through Tucson two or three days earlier.

I was frantic. Texas was a huge state. Where would I begin to look for him? Why did Dave go to Texas? He didn't have any family or friends there as far as I knew. Now his only family had been taken away from him. I made a few phone calls to animal shelters around Dallas and Houston, but no one could help me.

More than half a dozen years later, I still wonder what happened to Dave and Pixel. The practice of allowing hawkers to sell newspapers on the medians has been outlawed, and the homeless men who used to do this as their means of support have moved on. Perhaps Dave and Pixel moved on as well. Maybe they got away and were reunited. Or maybe the drifter who told Tony the story was wrong. But to this day, whenever I drive by the corner in northwest Tucson where Dave and Pixel used to sell newspapers, I still expect to see them there.

Koko

There's a proverb that says, "Fear makes the wolf bigger than he is." Becky Blanton knows something about fear, and the wolf, and what it takes to make the wolf disappear.

Becky graduated from the police academy in 1983, and part of her training had involved donning padded protective gear and learning how to manage dogs when they attack. She eventually left the police force and returned to school in the early 1990s to become a veterinary technician. After graduation, she went to work for a large veterinary practice, where she thoroughly enjoyed her

work and was exposed to and handled dogs of all temperaments on a daily basis.

So, when a good friend asked her to help with her Rottweiler after it had been injured in a fight, Becky didn't
hesitate. Becky knew the dog well, and she also knew how
to approach and touch an injured animal. But for just a
second, the Rottweiler caught Becky off guard and lunged
at her as she knelt in front of him. It was the second that
made all the difference.

When Becky arrived at the emergency room, the doctors discovered that she had been brutally attacked. One
of the physicians told her she was fortunate that her
throat had not been torn out, because the Rottweiler
had certainly come close. Becky had been gnawed from
her head down to her waist: her face, shoulders, breasts,
arms, and torso. Although the doctors were able to eventually repair the damage done to Becky's body, the attack
left deep scars on her emotional health.

"Nearly overnight I transformed from a woman who
had worked with aggressive police dogs and who handled
dogs every day as a veterinary technician into someone
who had panic attacks whenever I saw a dog," Becky
recalls. "I went to great lengths to avoid being anywhere

near a dog—on the street, in a park, anywhere. I felt like my fear was controlling my life."

Because of her new fear, Becky found it impossible to continue her work as a vet technician so she quit and went to work for a newspaper. Living in fear was not Becky's style, however, and about six months after the attack, she contacted a friend who ran a nonprofit Rottweiler rescue organization and asked if she could foster a few puppies so she could learn to overcome her fear of dogs, especially Rottweilers. At first the experiment created a lot of anxiety for Becky, but after a few weeks she felt more at ease with the puppies—although not completely. When homes were located for the puppies, Becky agreed to take another dog, a one-year-old female named Koko.

Koko had been rescued from an abusive environment, and she was timid and very underweight when Becky first saw her. As Becky recalls, at first she was terrified of Koko, and it was difficult to know who was more afraid or whom. When Becky brought Koko home, a cloud of wariness hung over the household until they got used to each other. During the first week of their breaking-in process, Becky took Koko to a veterinarian to have her

Koko in Becky's van

spayed; the vet announced that Koko was pregnant, but that because of her condition, the puppies could not be saved.

"It's strange, but I think the two of us began to bond then, like we were both in mourning," says Becky. "The experience of Koko losing her puppies alleviated much of the fear that I felt."

Becky and Koko soon settled into a routine of early-morning walks before Becky went to work at the newspaper and playtime in the evenings and on weekends.

Koko put on weight, blossoming from the scrawny forty-five pounds she weighed when Becky first got her to a healthy sixty-five. Her timidness seemed to disappear, as did Becky's fears and anxiety.

After working at the newspaper for about two years, Becky decided to leave and start a newspaper of her own in Washington State. She felt in control of her life and greatly enjoyed her work. Her stories, focusing on environmental issues, were extremely outspoken and controversial—so much so that it wasn't unusual for outraged citizens to roar into her office to express their views. Those were times that she was glad to have Koko with her to help keep the peace.

"Having a Rottie behind the counter when someone was shouting had a way of keeping things under control," she says, but over time even Koko's protective stares didn't stop the bomb threats. At that point, Becky decided she had had enough. She packed up Koko and a few belongings and moved to Denver, where she quickly got a job as the editor of a newspaper. She also decided to pursue another interest—photography—and began making extra money as a freelancer with Koko at her side.

Her joy was short-lived, however, when her father

died unexpectedly. "His death hit me hard," she says. "I became depressed and felt confused, and suddenly I didn't want to be tied down to a nine-to-five job anymore. I just wanted to be free." Becky quit her job, bought a van, and pursued freelance photography in earnest. It didn't pay the bills, unfortunately, and she and Koko, along with a cat named Roland, soon were homeless.

"I was homeless for eighteen months," says Becky. "I worked full-time, but I couldn't find an apartment that I could afford or one that would take a dog and a cat, and it was unthinkable for me to be without Koko and Roland, so we lived in the van." Becky remembers some of the "three-dog night" situations, when it was so cold "you needed three dogs to keep warm. Koko literally kept me warm. It was so cold, the tires froze to the pavement."

Becky's depression worsened so much that she wanted to commit suicide. "But Koko kept me going. She needed me and I truly needed her. I would not be alive today if it had not been for her."

After eighteen months of living out of the van, Becky, Koko, and Roland eventually found a place to call their own. Becky runs her freelance publishing business from the apartment, and Koko lies as her feet. When Becky takes to the road in her van, Koko goes with her.

"My friend who has the Rottweiler rescue organization says I saved Koko from a terrible life. Well, I think Koko saved me many times over, and she continues to save me. I'm grateful for her every day of my life."

The Only Thing to
Fear Is Fear Itself

Debbie Jacobs

I always thought I knew a lot about dogs because I had lived with them since I was three years old. But one dog showed me that I still had a lot to learn, not only about dogs, but about myself as well. Sunny forced me to really pay attention to dogs and how they communicate, and especially how important it is to try to decipher what dogs are telling us. All of these positive things are the result of taking in a dog who started life under circumstances that had DEAD END written all over them.

It all started in September 2005; Hurricane Katrina had just hit the Gulf coast and left its path of devastation across Louisiana and the surrounding region. At the time I was a volunteer with a local chapter of the Humane Society in Vermont, and when the call went out for volunteers to help with the rescue efforts in the hurricane-affected areas, I packed my bags.

They say that tragedy brings out the best in people, and it certainly was true during the animal rescue operations I participated in at the Humane Society of Louisiana's Camp Katrina in Tylertown, Mississippi, in the Katrina aftermath. Hundreds of volunteers from all over the country dug in and gave their all for the animals. But unfortunately, tragedies also bring out predators, and one example raised its head while I was down south.

Humane Society workers and other animal rescue volunteers heard about a facility called Every Dog Needs a Home, which was run by Tammy and William Hanson in Gamaliel, Arkansas. This alleged animal sanctuary had taken in more than one hundred dogs that had been victims of Hurricanes Katrina and Rita. Suspicions of wrongdoing by the Hansons prompted the sheriff's department to conduct a helicopter flyover of the property on Friday, October 21, 2005, and what they saw was troubling and prompted a search by the authorities. What they found was heartbreaking.

An estimated 477 dogs were on the property. Five were found dead, some in garbage bags, and about fifty dogs were running free. There were various dog runs and dog pens at the facility, and the largest enclosure had only two dog houses to accommodate more than fifty dogs in the pen. Trash was strewn everywhere, and among the garbage were dozens of cages with dogs locked inside. From the level of filth in the cages, it was apparent the dogs had rarely, if ever, left their metal prisons.

The Hansons were eventually charged with more than twenty counts of animal cruelty and various other felonies. After being charged, however, they fled and were only finally apprehended in late September 2009 and are now awaiting a trial.

What came out of this horrifying situation for me was a dog I eventually named Sunny. When I first saw Sunny at Camp Katrina in November 2005, he was a puppy, about nine or ten months old, hiding in the back of a cage. The best that any of the rescue workers could figure was that this Border collie mix had been born at Every Dog Needs a Home, along with several siblings.

After completing my week of volunteering, I flew back to Vermont after making arrangements for Sunny to follow as soon as he was healthy enough to fly. I had been assured by rescue workers that although Sunny was fearful of people, he was not aggressive. It was my intention at the time to keep Sunny just as long as it took for me to find a rescue group in Vermont, or nearby, to take him.

I counted the days until Sunny was to arrive and was thrilled when his plane finally set down. Sunny, on the other hand, was absolutely terrified. When we got home, it immediately became obvious that housebreaking him was going to be a huge undertaking. As soon as I touched him, he defecated on the floor and then ran into a corner in a room off the back of the kitchen. I could not put a collar or leash on him in order to lead him outdoors to relieve himself, and he would not respond to any of my commands or pleading. I tried to hold back the tears as I watched this poor dog tremble.

For an entire month, Sunny refused to leave the room to go outside, so I had to put down newspapers and keep cleaning up after him until he became slightly more at ease around me. I would talk to him in a calm voice every time I went into the room, which was many times a day, and when his anxiety level had gone down I let him watch while my other dog played with and retrieved tennis balls. I was gratified to see from his alert expression that he was interested!

Finally I was able to put a harness on Sunny and pull him outside. He panicked so badly that he tried to run away, and I felt terrible, but I was persistent. Every day, for weeks, I gently pulled him outside. My vet recommended an antidepressant, which helped reduce his anxiety and made it easier for him to learn. During this time I came to the realization that Sunny was not adoptable. Nothing can change the fundamental damage to the brain caused by a lack of socialization during a dog's early years, and Sunny had been traumatized for most of his first year, which was spent caged up at the Hansons' in Arkansas. I had a fearful dog on my hands, and I needed to find some help.

I turned to the Internet, bookstores, veterinarians, and professional dog handlers and trainers. One popular line of thinking about fearful dogs is that they may "come around," but as I soon learned, this often is not the case. Yet, the more I looked for advice on how to handle and train Sunny, the more frustrated I became. Although

Debbie Jacobs

there was lots of information about how to train dogs, there was very little about how dogs learn, and this seemed to me to be the key to helping to defuse Sunny's fear.

What I learned is that fearful dogs need to be taught in a fashion similar to how children with special learning issues are taught. You can't apply any one system—say, phonetics or the whole-language approach—until you see what inspires them and motivates them as individuals and how they react to different situations. I believed that if I understood how Sunny would best connect with what I wanted to teach him, I would have a much better chance of defusing his fear and teaching him commands.

That's when I decided that I needed to take matters into my own hands and put together all the information I could find on fearful dogs. I went to a local community college and learned how to put together a website of my own (www.fearfuldogs.com), and eventually I completed an e-book, *A Guide to Living and Working with a Fearful Dog*, that helps other people who have fearful dogs.

One approach that has been used by some canine trainers and handlers is to force the dogs to face their fears, that is, make the dog deal with fearful situations so it will become desensitized to them. This is sometimes referred to as a "flooding" or "exposure" technique, in which you force a dog to perform a behavior again and again. Although the dog may eventually "get" the behavior, for many this only increases their anxiety and eventually they bite.

I knew the flooding approach would not work with Sunny. What works with Sunny is a positive approach: I allow him to be in situations where he feels comfortable and safe and then I gradually add other elements, such as new people or new activities. One thing Sunny loves is other dogs, and I discovered that if Sunny was going to learn to feel safe around people other than me, he first needed to have other dogs around him.

Over time, I learned how to anticipate Sunny's behaviors and moods in everyday situations and how to manage them. For example, I don't give him an opportunity to display a wrong behavior, like growling at a stranger or running away, because I don't let strangers get that close to him. Basically, when you have a fearful dog, you are always in training mode. I guess I can liken it to having a special-needs child: You go on with your life and love and enjoy your child, but you are always watchful and vigilant, looking for things in the environment that may trigger a negative response.

After living with me for more than two years, Sunny is now generally happy, playful, and well trained. However, to this day, Sunny is still uncomfortable around my husband. Whenever I have to leave town for a few days, Sunny is not happy about being left with him, but they have established a respectful truce. Sunny also remains afraid of other people, but he is less afraid than he used to be. Unlike Sunny, many dogs that are afraid of people were not physically abused but rather were not given the opportunity to experience different people and different situations during the time of their life when their brain was developing the capacity to feel safe and comfortable with novel experiences.

Fearful dogs like Sunny can be a challenge, but the rewards are enormous. I have watched a cowering but beautiful dog blossom into a loving, happy, less anxious companion. He has taught me how to be patient and the importance of being calm, and he puts a smile on my face every day.

I am fortunate that I work at home and that we live in a rural area. I don't think Sunny could adjust to an urban situation, but here he doesn't need to be a social butterfly. Here, without dozens of distractions, I have the luxury of gradually trying to understand what Sunny is saying to me when he behaves in a certain way. I can't imagine maneuvering Sunny down a busy city street with car horns blaring, crowded sidewalks, jackhammers, lights, and traffic. Heck, it's enough to scare me at times!

The Four-Legged
Family

When Larry and Sue got married in 2003, they were both twenty-six years old and had every intention of starting a traditional family, which, in their minds, meant two children. The plan was for Sue to get pregnant by the time she was thirty and then wait three to four more years before having a second child. She is a commercial graphic artist, and planned to work with a large firm until their first child was born and then to work freelance at home until both children were in school full-time.

Larry is an attorney, and on several occasions they'd

told me that their "life plan" was to buy a house that would allow them to have two home offices, one for Sue and one for Larry, who wanted to open a home practice someday. Together with their plans for children, they were confident that they'd orchestrated the next few decades of their lives and that they would turn out as they envisioned.

One year into their marriage, as they were still settling into a new four-bedroom home that fulfilled their dream for home offices, they found a dog wandering in the yard early one morning. It looked like a black Lab and German shepherd mix, about forty pounds or so, with one ear up and one ear down. They fell in love immediately. Sue had grown up with dogs all her life and desperately wanted one again. This one seemed to be heaven-sent: no tags, no license, no collar, and very friendly.

Larry, however, was resistant. He had never had a dog as a child and said he hadn't planned on bringing one into his life now, especially since they both worked and it wasn't part of their "master plan." Sue pleaded for a compromise: She would try to find the rightful owner and, if that failed, they would keep him. After all, their house had a fence around the backyard and a porch where the dog could stay if it rained; they had the perfect environment for him while they were at work. Larry reluctantly agreed.

I helped Sue contact the local dog shelter and Humane Society to see if anyone had reported the dog missing and we posted signs in the neighborhood. As a dear old friend of the couple and an avid dog lover myself, I shared Sue's delight when a full week passed and no one contacted us. Rightful ownership was now theirs, and they named the dog Midas.

A trip to the vet revealed that Midas was a neutered male about one year old, who apparently had suffered an injury to his front right leg at some point, as he walked with a slight limp. Otherwise he was healthy. Sue and I began lavishing him with toys, a matching leash and collar, and doggie treats, while Larry just shook his head at Sue. "If you do this with a dog, I can just imagine how you'll spoil our kids," he said.

About this time, Sue and Larry decided to concentrate on starting their human family, but after six months of effort Sue still was not pregnant. When they consulted Sue's gynecologist, she felt that her endometriosis, which she had experienced since her early twenties, could be preventing conception, as it is a known cause of infertil-

ity. Larry and Sue were determined to keep trying, however, but as her thirty-second birthday came and went,
they still were not pregnant.

Just after that birthday the couple was presented
with another canine opportunity. One of Sue's cowork-
ers, Sarah, found two dogs abandoned in a box by the
road, and she asked Sue if she wanted one of them; she
would keep the other. The little ball of black and white fur
with the huge feet melted all of our hearts immediately,
and Sue vigorously campaigned to Larry to accept the
adorable female dog into their household as a companion for Midas. Again, he reluctantly agreed, and Marbles
joined their family.

Sarah also instigated the next canine change in their
lives. She was a volunteer with a local animal rescue organization, and she was part of a team of other dedicated
individuals who found foster homes for dogs destined for
euthanasia. She also headed a committee that secured
low cost spay and neuter services for people who were in
low-income brackets.

One day, after Larry and Sue had been trying for
about eighteen months to get pregnant, Sarah called Sue
with desperation in her voice: She needed someone to
foster a two-year-old Chow mix named Barney who

would be put down the next day if she didn't find a temporary home for him. Would Sue do it? "I can't take another foster right now myself, because my mother is moving in," she said. "And I already have six dogs."

Sue knew that Sarah must be in a real bind because she always stepped up in a doggie emergency. With trepidation, she brought Barney into the house that night after work and waited for Larry to come home. The minute he walked in the front door, Barney ran to him and looked at him expectedly. "What's this?" Larry looked tired and grumpy, and Sue thought to herself, *this isn't going to go over well.*

Sue told him Barney was just a foster and that they didn't have to keep him. To her surprise, Larry bent down and scratched the dog behind the ears. "He reminds me of my grandfather's dog, Blue," he said.

"I didn't know your grandfather had a dog."

Larry stood up. "Yeah, well we weren't allowed to have a dog, because my mother didn't want one in the house. Too much hair, she always said. But whenever I went to my grandfather's house, I got to play with Blue. I really loved that dog. Then one day Blue got hit by a car while I was playing ball with him. I guess I always felt like his death was my fault. So I've been afraid to get attached to another dog again ever since."

It was the most Larry had ever talked about a dog, and Sue knew right away that Barney would be staying with them. He instantly became Larry's dog, as if he knew that Larry needed him in order to resolve his old conflicts. Soon after they accepted Barney into their home, Sue became interested in the work Sarah was doing with the spay/neuter program. Sue asked her to help register people for the next free spay/neuter day her organization was sponsoring. Sue went to one of the group's planning meetings and was shocked by the statistics that one of the other volunteers, Judy, was relaying: Approximately 10 million dogs and cats are euthanized annually in the United States; more than half of all dogs that enter animal shelters are put down.

"I feel like I'm making a difference when I help with these free spay/neuter days," Judy said. "It doesn't make a huge dent in the problem, but every little bit helps when it comes to reducing companion animal overpopulation."

As Sue approached her thirty-third birthday, she and Larry took stock of their lives: They had discussed in vitro fertilization, but the entire process seemed too emotionally, physically, and financially draining. Sue was doing well in her career and had even taken on some freelance projects that she did after work and on weekends, and Larry was up for partner. They just didn't have the time or the energy for such a huge undertaking.

They resigned themselves to two options: adoption, or no children at all. At the same time, however, their enthusiasm for having children was waning as their involvement with their three dogs (they had kept Barney) and Sue's participation with the animal rescue group increased. At night and on weekends, they found themselves with "the kids": taking the dogs on hikes and training them to do all sorts of tricks and tasks. Sue told me that, along with her work and time volunteering with the animal rescue group, she felt fulfilled. Larry expressed a similar sentiment: They felt like a family and thought less and less about starting a new one.

On their six-year wedding anniversary, Larry and Sue adopted two more dogs: two beagle-mix sisters named Molly and Malinda. Their family had grown to the point that one of us needed to work at home, so Sue finally started her freelance graphic art business in a spare bedroom. Larry had a home office, although he still worked at a firm in town. They had happily and gradually created their family, albeit a nontraditional one, far from the one they had envisioned six years earlier.

Today they still foster dogs for the animal rescue group, so along with Midas, Marbles, Barney, Molly, and Malinda, they often have several other temporary family members. Sue volunteers time to do fund-raising to support the free spay/neuter program, and Larry does pro bono work for several animal rescue groups in town. Their new plan, before they turn forty, is to buy a small farm or a house with a few acres so they'll have room for their growing family. Yes, they want more "children."

Some of their friends say they might regret not having a "real" family or "real" children, but they feel that their family is very real and satisfying to them. They may decide to adopt someday, but if they do, that child or children will be welcomed into a thriving, loving family of parents and dogs, a family that brings both of them incredible pleasure.

Chet

Elizabeth Zimels

When I first saw Chet at the Humane Society in Michigan, he was about four months old and too young to walk on a leash. I fell in love with the spaniel-dachshund mix immediately and would have brought him home on the spot had I not had to "sleep on it" because I needed the landlord's permission for a dog in the house where I was living. I was so afraid someone else would take Chet overnight, and as soon as the landlord gave his okay, I rushed down to the Humane Society and was grateful he was still there.

I was in veterinary school at the time, between my first and second years. I practiced a few of the techniques

I was learning in school on Chet, although at no time did I hurt the little guy. If he could have talked he probably would have said I hurt his pride. I practiced palpations, measured him for angular limb deformities, and made him stand still so I could figure out where all the internal organs were from the outside. He took all of my position-ings and gentle proddings with wary patience, and I'm sure the treats I carried in my pocket for such occasions helped motivate him to cooperate.

Throughout my years in veterinary school, Chet was my helpmate and my inspiration. He got along great with my boyfriend, who became my fiancé during my fourth and final year of school, and I envisioned the three of us moving in together and me going into practice after graduation.

Immediately after graduation, however, plans chan-ged. My fiancé and I called off the wedding, and so I packed up Chet and a few belongings and moved to the East Coast. I was fortunate to quickly find a job in a thriving practice, but I was still in a funk because of my breakup. I believe I probably would not have been able to get up every day if it had not been for Chet, who needed to be walked every morning. Maybe I thought I was doing him a favor, but in reality he was helping me get through those first few months—new job, new city, no fiancé—by always being there for me at the beginning and the end of each day.

At first I was overwhelmed by the demands of my new job. It took months to get used to the diverse personalities and behaviors of the steady stream of dogs, cats, and their owners who came into the office. Chet was the one steady thing in my life—he was easygoing and undemanding, and his devotion was unconditional.

I eventually reached a stage in my life when I wanted to give back to the community, so I enrolled Chet as a therapy dog with The Good Dog Foundation in New York. Chet was eleven years old by that time, and although I had never trained him for obedience, he did well during the training sessions.

Chet's build did not make him a great candidate for therapy dog services: His short, stubby legs and long body made it impossible for him to reach patients in their beds. But it was quickly obvious that Chet's tranquil personality was a big asset; nurses could drop trays and he would hardly jump, and he had a calming effect on psychiatric patients. Chet also had another great asset for therapy: He was a goofy-looking dog, and he made people smile. He had always made me smile, and now he was doing it for people who were lonely, depressed, in pain, frightened, and confused. What better gift could this little dog bring?

Eventually, Chet developed bad arthritis and I treated him with anti-inflammatory drugs, glucosamine, and acupuncture. As the months passed, it became harder and harder for Chet to walk. Then one day when I came home, I discovered that Chet had urinated on the floor and could not get up anymore. He was fifteen and a half years old, and it was clear to me that it was time to let him go.

Chet wasn't noble or heroic; he didn't make headlines or have his picture on dog food bags or magazine covers. But he was a steady soul in my life. He also inspired me to give back, because he had given me so much.

So, in honor of Chet, I volunteered to spay and neuter dozens of feral cats that had been gathered up as part of a local nonprofit's neuter-and-release program. That was a onetime event. My intention is to keep giving back every day. One way I can do that is to answer the question I get asked often—"What kind of dog is the best to get?"—by encouraging people to rescue a dog from a shelter. I quickly quell their protests and explain that most shelters screen dogs for compatibility, so you can put in a request for a specific gender, size, breed, and age.

Perhaps even more important is my attempt to convey to people the problems that are created when humans fail to sterilize their companion animals. We euthanize millions of dogs and cats every year in the United States, not because they are sick and dying, but because there are too many of them, unwanted, abandoned, and guilty of nothing except that they were born.

I am truly grateful Chet was born. I hope everyone who brings a dog into their life has an experience as wonderful as mine.

A Matter of Trust

Sassafras Lowrey

I t's no exaggeration to say that dogs have defined my
life. Ever since I was a small child, I have felt drawn
to dogs in ways that didn't make sense to other people. When other kids were playing games with one another, I wanted to be with dogs. As a child of the 1980s, I
watched an endless number of *Lassie* reruns. Any show,
movie, or documentary that had dogs in it, I watched.

One reason for this obsession with watching shows
that had dogs in them was that I did not have a dog
as a young child. After I was in elementary school for a
few years, my parents finally acquiesced to my constant

whining for a dog and we got one. This stopped the whining but not the obsession. I read every book about dogs that I could find, and most of my spare time was spent with my dog. I somehow managed to turn any conversation around to include discussion about dogs, which didn't endear me to a great many people.

But that was okay with me. I appreciated the honesty, trust, and loyalty that dogs so freely gave. I was part of a highly dysfunctional family, and these character traits were not ones I experienced often from people. I also lived in a semirural area, which didn't allow me to socialize a great deal except when I was in school. I was never comfortable with girls my own age. They wanted to talk about boys and I wanted to talk about dogs. It is little wonder that I didn't have friends. Since no one was as well-versed in dog knowledge and trivia as I was, I managed to keep to myself quite a bit.

As a teenager, I isolated myself from people to become immersed in dog training and competition. All of my spare time was spent training dogs and then getting them ready for canine sports competitions such as obedience and tracking. My real passion, however, was dog agility training, and I rose to the top level of that sport in

Mercury and Sassafras

my area and age division. The best times I remember as a teenager were those hours I spent with my dogs.

My world came crashing down at age seventeen when I came out as lesbian to my family. My parents immediately banned me and my dogs from the house, and I went to live with my dog trainer, her husband, and their nine dogs. They assumed I had family troubles and were happy to take me in, but I didn't tell them exactly why I had been banished. Of course, it hurt to be thrown out of my childhood home, but I still had my dogs and I was able to continue doing what I loved while finishing my senior year of high school. I dedicated my time to training the dogs and going to dog shows.

That high only lasted about one year. My trainer and her husband learned that I was a lesbian, and once again I found myself being thrown out of a house because of my sexual orientation. But this time, the blow was twofold: I could not take my dogs, Magnet and Aristotle, with me. I was given forty-eight hours to clear out and I had to sign over the dogs' AKC papers to my trainer. Magnet was in intensive training and had just begun to compete; Aristotle was ready to retire from the circuit. My maternal grandparents agreed to take Aristotle, but since I did not have a relationship with them, the only solace I had was knowing that Aristotle would have a safe, loving home and good care. I could handle the next chapter in my life—living on the streets—but it was no place for my beautiful dogs.

For many people, being homeless is devastating. But for me, having to give up my dogs was much more traumatic than not having a home. I also lost my connection with the many people in the dog training and show circuits, and the combination of these two losses left me crushed.

Over the next few months I struggled to get my life back in order. I felt a compelling need to stay connected with dogs in some way, so I got a job at a dog wash. Eventually I enrolled in college and majored in women's studies. While in college I worked part-time at a doggie day care center, and the nearly daily interaction with the dogs left me longing for the day when I could have a dog of my own again.

During my second year of college I had an accident and severely hurt my wrist, which made it impossible for me to continue working at the doggie day care. Still hoping to keep a dog connection, I began writing for different dog publications as a freelance writer. At about the same time I rented a small apartment and felt ready to take the plunge and share it with canines. I went to the local animal shelter and adopted Mercury, a dachshund-Chihuahua mix. Although it was wonderful to have a dog in my life again, in the beginning I was also terrified that something would happen to him and that I would lose him. There was no logical reason for this fear, yet it persisted for about six months. As my anxieties gradually subsided, I added Cosmo, a Border collie mix, to the household.

Today, about eight years later, I still share my home with Mercury, but we lost Cosmo three years ago. As I think back, dogs have always been a vibrant and unifying thread in my life. Although some important people turned against me over the years, there were always dogs somewhere in my life to bring me back, to ground me. In some way they taught me that it's okay to trust people, that not everyone is terrible.

Some people wear their hearts on their sleeves. I wear tributes to my dogs and their loving lessons on my body. Across my upper right arm I had seven paw prints tattooed to represent each of the dogs who have touched my heart and whom my life has been intertwined with. On my calf is an agility course, which memorializes the times when dog agility competitions played such a significant part of my life by helping me accumulate the strength and fortitude to keep moving forward every day. Around the tattooed course are the words "I could have missed the pain, but I'd of had to miss the dance." On my left biceps is a portrait of Mercury in the form of an angel statue/gargoyle.

I have used my body as a canvas for permanent inked monuments to dogs and special moments in my life. To this day, dogs continue to guide how I see the world. They have taught me a permanent truth—they taught me to trust.

Closing Tails

Humans Helping Dogs

The stories in this section have been about how dogs have inspired or helped people make life-changing choices, accomplish major goals, and better understand themselves and what their place is in this world. Here we turn the tables and discuss what you can do to make a positive difference in the lives of dogs. If you have thought about giving back to the canine community in ways other than working with therapy or service dogs, then read on. We talk about how you can volunteer for dogs in different capacities, and also what it takes to care for dogs that have special needs—those that have physical disabilities and/or health problems that require extra patience, care, and understanding.

Volunteer for the Dogs

"I walked into my local animal shelter to look for a dog for my kids," says Robin, a forty-year-old mother of two, "and I walked out not only with a dog but with a commitment to volunteer for the dogs." The thousands of animal shelters, animal protection organizations, and animal rescue groups across the United States are typically in need of volunteer help. Volunteer jobs can range from walking dogs to helping organize fund-raisers to staffing a booth at an animal fair. The needs and requirements of each animal organization vary, so you will need to contact them to learn about their volunteer programs. Most of the organizations have websites, where you can often learn much about the group even before you contact them. Check online under the headings "animal shelter," "humane society," and "animal control" for the organizations in your area.

Volunteering to help dogs can be a very rewarding

Volunteering to help dogs can be a rewarding experience.

experience. "I never realized how much love you can get from dogs," said Ursula, who helps clean cages and walks dogs for a rescue group in her city. "I feel like they are my dogs. They know me and wait for me. I volunteer two afternoons a week, and I have the greatest time. A friend asked me how I could stand cleaning cages, and I said that these dogs give such unconditional love to me, they deserve to be clean and cared for. It's a privilege to help them."

People who volunteer to help dogs and other animals mention some of the benefits, including:

- Knowing you are part of a community of hundreds of thousands of other people who are helping to make the lives of dogs a little easier
- Making new friends, both four-legged and two-legged
- Learning new skills
- Learning new things about yourself. Volunteering can be especially enlightening for young people, for whom this may be their first volunteer experience.

Special-needs Dogs

A special-needs dog is one that is difficult to adopt out because it has a medical condition or illness (e.g., blindness, deafness, loss of limb[s], diabetes, thyroid disorder, epilepsy), is elderly, or has an emotional problem (e.g., aggressiveness, extreme shyness, fearfulness). Emotional problems can be more challenging to manage than physical conditions: While physical or medical conditions can usually be treated with medication, medical procedures, or devices (e.g., scooters), emotional problems are often the result of neglect, abuse, or lack of socialization and are harder to treat and understand. Because dogs can't tell us how they feel, we are left to decipher their emotional states from their behavior.

In some cases, dogs that fall into the special-needs category are considered unadoptable and end up being euthanized or spending their remaining days in a shelter or rescue facility, where they are cared for by staff and volunteers.

By definition, special-needs dogs require special attention. Some special-needs dogs are included in this book: Frankie, who has a custom-made scooter to substitute for her missing back legs, in section three; and Sunny, the fearful dog, in the story, "The Only Thing to Fear Is Fear Itself," in section two. Like a special-needs child, dogs who have physical and/or emotional challenges typically require more time, patience, and, in many cases, financial support. Therefore, accepting a dog with special needs into your home is a weighty decision.

Fortunately, there are many resources for people who have dogs that have physical and medical conditions.

Scooters, lifts, orthotics, and ramps have been designed to help those with physical needs, while medications and therapies such as acupuncture, herbal remedies, massage, and physical therapy can also offer relief for both physical and emotional conditions. There are also organizations that offer support for people who take a special-needs dog into their homes and their hearts. See the Resources on the following pages of this section for some of these groups.

Resources

Adopt-a-Pet.com

www.adoptapet.com/animal-shelters

This website helps you find animal shelters in your area and covers all fifty states.

**Aggressive Behavior in Dogs
Discussion Group**

http://pets.groups.yahoo.com/group/agbeh/

This group includes 3,385 members. Of them, 700 are experienced dog trainers and the remaining 2,685 are pet owners from all around the world who have an interest in canine behavior and training. This group is conducted as an educational forum. You'll find discussions on how to modify the behavior of dogs that sometimes exhibit aggressiveness toward dogs and/or toward people. Aggressive behaviors oftentimes arise from dogs' fears or anxieties. Harsh training and physical punishments are not advised because they may make the problems worse.

Animal Hospice Compassionate Crossings

www.animalhospice.org

Not a place but a philosophy that promotes healing through shared understanding. Animal Hospice Compassionate Crossings offers services to anyone anticipating or coping with the loss of an animal companion. Volunteers visit by mail, by e-mail, by telephone, or in person.

Deaf Dog Education Action Fund

http://deafdogs.org

A website that offers information and resources on deaf dogs and how to care for them.

HandicappedPets.com

http://handicappedpets.com/www/index.php

A website that offers support for caretakers of injured, handicapped, and elderly companion animals. The site provides articles, product information, and other services.

Humane Society of America

http://hsus.org/pets/pet_adoption_information/adopting_
from_an_animal_shelter.html

See the article titled "Adopting from an Animal Shelter or Rescue Group."

Little Angels Rescue

www.littleangelsrescue.org/adoption/senior.special.needs.
dog.htm

A website that offers information and resources on caring for senior and other special-needs dogs.

Old Dog Haven

www.olddoghaven.org

A nonprofit group that provides a network of homes for dog assisted living and hospice care. They also place senior dogs.

Petfinder.com

www.petfinder.com

A database of several hundred thousand adoptable companion animals across North America; plus, pet care tips, classified ads, pet forums, and much more. Search for a dog by breed, size, gender, age, and location.

Pets with Disabilities

www.petswithdisabilities.org/adopt.html

This nonprofit organization is both a shelter and an adoption placement aid for animals that have been injured or disabled by illness. It also provides support and resources for people who have disabled companion animals. Their motto is, "Because their spirits aren't broken."

Shy-K9s Discussion Group

http://pets.groups.yahoo.com/group/shy-k9s/

The shy-k9s mailing list is for the discussion of shy, fearful, and/or fear-aggressive dogs and positive solutions to their problems.

The Senior Dogs Project

www.srdogs.com

Lots of resources for how to care for a senior dog.

BOOKS

Donaldson, Jean. *Fight! A Practical Guide to the Treatment of Dog-Dog Aggression.* New York: Kinship Communications, 2004.

A practical guide to the treatment of dog-dog aggression. Includes descriptions of common types of aggression, prognoses,

EVERY DOG HAS A GIFT

remedial socialization, on-leash manners training, proximity sensi-
tivity, play style and skills, resource guarding, and prevention.

McConnell, Patricia B., Ph.D. *Cautious*
Canine: How to Help Dogs Conquer Their
Fears, **2nd ed. Wenatchee, WA: Dogwise**
Publishing, 2005.

This booklet provides a step-by-step dog training program
of desensitizing and classical counterconditioning. Covered are
details related to identifying exactly what triggers your dog, creating a step-by-step treatment plan, monitoring your progress, and
understanding why you need to treat the fear and not just your
dog's reaction to the fear.

McConnell, Patricia, and Karen London.
Feisty Fido: Help for the Leash-Aggressive Dog,
2nd ed. Wenatchee, WA: Dogwise Publishing,
2009.

Practical information about positive ways to teach dogs how to
walk politely walk past other dogs without causing a scene. Written for both novices and professionals, it includes tips on prevention and handling emergency situations. Humane and upbeat.

142

3

kids + dogs = magic

Jessica

Deborah Mitchell

I first saw Jessica as I was climbing the stairs of an old house in Lawrenceville, New Jersey. She was attempting to hide behind an upholstered chair that stood at an angle to the left of the top of the staircase. All I could see was her rear end, golden hair flecked with white, and it was shaking. Rebecca, the woman who had placed the ad, and whom I had spoken to on the phone just an hour earlier, greeted me with an apologetic look on her face.

"She's a little scared, like I said on the phone," she explained as she stepped aside for me. "But she's really a great dog, never heard her bark, seems fine on a leash."

I went around the corner of the chair so I could see the dog's face. She looked like a Shetland sheepdog–collie mix, with a long snout that she had placed between her extended front legs. She didn't raise her head but looked up at me, and her doe eyes looked frightened. My heart melted immediately.

"Like I said, I would have taken her to the Humane Society, but I was afraid no one would want her because of her leg," Rebecca explained. "But she gets around fine."

Rebecca had told me much of the dog's story over the phone. About a week earlier, in the first week of January, a neighbor had asked Rebecca if she knew anything about the people across the street. It appeared that the young couple had left in the middle of the night to avoid paying the back rent they owed, and they had left a dog chained to a doghouse—hardly adequate shelter in the cold January weather. Even worse, there was no food bowl in sight, and the water dish contained ice. The neighbor had contacted the landlord, who checked out the house and found that the people had indeed skipped out.

The landlord was ready to send the dog to a shelter, but Rebecca offered to take her.

"I never planned to keep her," she said. "But I felt so sorry for her, especially since she has only three legs. I can't afford to take her to the vet and all, but I've been feeding her and she eats good."

It took some time, but we were finally able to coax the dog out from behind the chair. She stood in the middle of the living room looking very uncomfortable and occasionally shaking as if in fear. I was able to examine the small stump that was where her hind leg would have been, and she did not protest. The stump appeared to be a birth defect or perhaps the remnant of surgical removal of the leg.

My reason for getting a dog was to keep Jamie company. Jamie was my six-year-old terrier mix, who weighed about twenty-five pounds. I had planned to get a dog about the same size, but this three-legged female was twice as big. Suddenly that requirement seemed senseless.

"I don't suppose you know her name," I asked Rebecca, and she shook her head no. That didn't matter, either; I had already chosen the name Jessica.

"Come here, girl," I said, and she let me slip a collar around her neck and then snap on a leash. She was quiet but she had her tail down and looked to still be on guard. I felt she wanted to crawl back behind the chair, but I had decided she was going home with me.

"I suppose I'll need to carry her down the stairs," I asked. "Did you carry her up?"

"No, she made it on her own," Rebecca replied, "but she was real slow. I was afraid she was going to fall."

I didn't think I could safely carry Jessica down the stairs, so I led her down slowly. Jessica nearly hopped from step to step to the bottom of the stairs. Once we were outside, she looked across the street at the house where she had been tied up. I assured her that she would never have to worry about that again.

Jamie and Jessica got acquainted quickly, with Jamie immediately establishing his territory and Jessica retiring behind the toilet in the master bathroom. My husband and I had several acres of wooded property around our house, and so I began walking Jessica around the property several times a day so she would become familiar with the area and with me. When I took both dogs, they pulled me in two different directions so they wouldn't have to deal with each other. All in all, it was a quiet truce.

I took Jessica to our vet, who took X-rays of her stump and her hips and told me that her three-leg status was apparently a birth defect. In any case, her lack of a left back leg didn't seem to bother her: She was a fast runner, and her balance was good when she stopped. The vet said she was otherwise in good health and was probably about three years old.

As the weather improved in the spring, I began taking Jessica to places where she could get socialized. One of our favorite spots, not far from our house, was a large county park where many people walked their dogs. One afternoon there was a festival in the park, and Jessica and I were taking in the smells and sounds. Jessica always drew attention to herself because of her missing leg, and because she still frightened easily, I was constantly mindful of people who wanted to reach out and pet her.

While we were listening to some bluegrass music, I noticed a young boy in a wheelchair who was seated about thirty or so feet away. He looked to be about eight or nine years old, and a woman, who was likely his mother, was standing behind the chair, chatting with someone. The boy, however, was staring hard at Jessica with a look of curiosity on his face. I noticed that he had a blanket draped over his lap, which wasn't surprising, given that it was a cool April day.

I glanced repeatedly at the boy until he caught my eye, and the first time he did, he quickly looked away. When our eyes met again, he smiled tentatively, and I immediately smiled back and slowly started walking toward him. His eyes lit up as we approached. It was then that I noticed there was only one shoe peeping out from under his blanket on the wheelchair's footrest.

"Hi, this is Jessica," I said, "and my name is Toni. Jessica is a little shy, but we thought we would come over and see you. Is that all right?" The boy's mother had turned to us by now and was smiling.

"Hi, I'm Jeannette," she said. "Bobbie loves dogs, and he's always saying he wants one, but we haven't de-cided what to do yet."

"What happened to her leg?" asked Bobbie. I ex-plained how Jessica had been born with just a stump where a real leg should be, and that she had adjusted very well, that she could run very fast, and that she loved to chase balls. Bobbie took in this all, then looked away.

"I can't run anymore." Bobbie said looking down at

his lap. "I don't have a leg anymore. If I had three legs like her then I could run, but I only have one so I can't."

I was unsure how to answer Bobbie, but his mother quickly saved the day by explaining how Bobbie had been in an automobile accident and lost his leg more than a year before. The plan was for Bobbie to get an artificial leg and start rehabilitation therapy. During my conversation with Jeannette, Bobbie had been quietly petting Jessica, who stood passively by his side. Rarely had I seen her this calm around a stranger, and especially one who was attached to a strange device.

I remarked to Jeannette how well Jessica and Bobbie seemed to be getting along, and Bobbie beamed. Suddenly I found myself asking Jeannette if they lived close by and how I would be happy to bring Jessica by to visit Bobbie sometime, if that was okay. It turned out that they lived only a few miles away from me, and we exchanged addresses and phone numbers. After Bobbie spent a bit more time petting and talking to Jessica, I said we had to leave but promised Bobbie we would come over soon.

Little did I know how soon that would be. Jeannette called me a day later, saying how Bobbie had not stopped talking about Jessica. "He has not been this animated in more than a year," she said, with what sounded like tears in her voice. "He has been depressed ever since the accident and, to tell you the truth, we've been really worried about him. We've taken him to a child psychologist and the doctor suggested antidepressants, but we hate to put him on drugs. Seeing Jessica seems to really perk him up. Would you mind bringing her over someday soon?"

I promised to visit the coming weekend, and Jessica and Bobbie spent hours together. They played fetch with a tennis ball, and I let Bobbie groom Jessica, which she loved. Then Bobbie started reading a book to her, and Jessica lay with her head between her front paws, looking like she was taking in the story.

As fate would have it, while Jessica and Bobbie's life seemed to be getting better, my personal life was getting worse. My husband filed for divorce after deciding he wanted to be with someone else, and we needed to sell the house. At the same time, the company I worked for downsized, and I found myself unemployed. Fortunately, I was quickly able to find another job that paid well but it involved a great deal of travel.

I was in a difficult position: I needed and wanted the job but I didn't know what to do with Jessica. My husband said he would take Jamie, who had been his dog before we got married. But he did not want Jessica, and I did not know what to do with her while I would be away on extended trips. When Jeannette learned of my dilemma, she immediately offered a suggestion: They would take Jessica, if it was okay with me.

"Jessica is so good for Bobbie," she said, "and we've grown so fond of her visits. And you could, of course, come and see her anytime you want to. We would love to make her part of our family."

Although the thought of giving Jessica away broke my heart, I also knew she would be going to the perfect home: one not only full of love, but one where she would be a continuing inspiration for Bobbie.

That was two years ago. I still visit Bobbie and Jessica several times a month when I'm in town. Bobbie has an artificial leg and is doing well in school. He's no longer depressed, and he has taken up golf with his father. Jessica goes to the practice range with Bobbie and his father, sitting quietly while they practice hitting balls.

Frankie:
Keep On Rolling!

Barbara Techel

Let's face it: We worry about our image. We worry about being too fat, too thin, too bald, too short, too tall. We want to fit in, to be liked, to have other people think well of us.

Dogs, on the other hand, don't seem to have this image problem. They seem to accept their lot in life and generally carry on, if at all possible, and often against what we might regard as incredible odds.

If we're different, especially in ways that are obvious—like being in a wheelchair, or having one arm, or having a birthmark on our face—we're afraid people will stare at us, make us feel uncomfortable, or perhaps even make inappropriate remarks. Generally, it is not the kind of attention we want to draw to ourselves.

So when my husband and I made the decision to fit Frankie, our six-year-old dachshund, with a wheelchair when she lost use of her back legs, I was apprehensive about bringing her out in public. What would people think? Would they think it was mean or cruel of me to subject her to living in this contraption? Would people laugh at her and me or make rude remarks?

Let me back up for a few moments to explain how Frankie came to be in her wheelchair, or, perhaps more accurately, a back-wheel cart. In 2006, my husband and I went on vacation and arranged for Frankie to stay in a kennel, one in which she had stayed on previous occasions. While at the kennel, Frankie, being the enthusiastic little girl that she is, jumped into her food dish, fell, and ruptured a disk in her back. She needed immediate surgery, and after the procedure her vets gave her a 30 percent chance of ever walking again. After three months of physical therapy, including swimming exercises in the bathtub at home, the vets determined that Frankie would never regain use of her back legs.

That's when my husband and I decided to buy a custom-built cart for Frankie that would support her back legs and allow her to walk normally using her front legs. Years ago, dogs that had injuries like Frankie's were typically euthanized, but today there are several manufacturers that make front-wheel and back-wheel carts and wheelchairs for physically challenged companion animals.

It didn't take long for Frankie to become accustomed to her new "legs." My apprehension about taking her out in public disappeared quickly as I found that most people, especially children, were fascinated with the dog on wheels. In fact, their profound interest soon convinced me that Frankie could be an ambassador for positive thinking and an example of how to accept and overcome challenges in life.

Suddenly I wanted everyone to see Frankie and to know her story, and one way to do that was to write a book, which I published in 2008, titled *Frankie the Walk 'N Roll Dog*. But writing the book and publishing it was only a small part of what became a much bigger picture, much grander than I ever could have imagined.

Frankie's life and mine became intimately entwined as we went to schools and hospitals, visiting with children, listening to their questions and comments, and simply allowing Frankie to work her magic. I soon discovered just how innocent, caring, and philosophic children can be.

"How come your dog has training wheels?" asked one young boy when we visited his classroom. No one had ever referred to the cart in that way before, and I realized that this child did not see Frankie as having a disability but simply as using a tool that allowed her to carry on, to "keep on rolling."

Another tool at Frankie's disposal is the Internet. Children always have so many questions to ask Frankie, and so, as a way to help children understand her message and learn about the Internet at the same time, I started a blog for her. Now children can send in their questions and then access the blog to see how she answered them. Teachers are very excited about their students using the Internet in this way.

Although it was my hope that, through our interactions with children and adults, Frankie and I would bring a message that said to "Keep on rolling" through life's challenges, I never imagined the form that some of those interactions would take and the opportunities that would arise.

So I was surprised when I was contacted by an ele-

Frankie

mentary school in Canada that was launching a pilot program that included lessons on compassion. One of the teachers had seen a video of Frankie on the Internet and thought Frankie could teach her students, and others in the school, a lot about compassion. She contacted me and asked if we would participate in their lessons via webcam and Skype.

This approach was new to me and very exciting. I learned from the teacher that by using my webcam, the children would see Frankie and me projected onto the wall of the gym as we talked to them and answered their questions. The sound would be piped through speakers that were placed around the gym, and when the children wanted to ask us a question, they would walk up to the computer, which has a built-in camera, and we would see the child.

The experience was an instant success. Frankie sat on my lap, and one by one the children walked up to the computer and asked us questions. One especially powerful question came from a young girl who looked very intense as she asked, "Since you have a handicapped dog, would you ever adopt another dog in wheels someday?" I had no trouble answering that question with

"Absolutely yes!" which was followed by the thought that this was an important message to give children about how it was all right to be different.

After the children met with Frankie and me for the first time, they decided they wanted to help other animals in need. Their enthusiasm resulted in the kids organizing a raffle, which they named in Frankie's honor—"Frankie the Walk 'N Roll Raffle." The raffle items included copies of the book I wrote about Frankie, as well as other items, and the children then chose a local animal agency to be the recipient of the proceeds.

Frankie's positive influence on children will clearly continue after this program ends and even when he is not physically present in a child's life. For example, I received a letter from a woman named Helen whose young daughter has cerebral palsy, which requires her to wear braces on her legs. Helen said that she had bought my book and had read it to her daughter, Claudia, the night before she had to begin wearing a new leg brace to bed. Wearing braces at all has been very difficult for the four-year-old girl, said Helen, and having to wear one to bed was something her daughter was finding difficult to accept. After Claudia listened to Frankie's story, however, and Helen explained how Frankie had learned to still have fun despite having to wear wheels, Claudia said, "I guess I have to wear my braces like Frankie."

That a dachshund ambassador in a wheelchair can teach such important life lessons gives me hope for the future of our children. Every day I see evidence that Frankie has touched another heart and helped another child see that all things are possible if you just keep on rolling. I know that's what Frankie has taught me.

If you'd like to read Frankie's blog, you can visit it at http://frankiethewalknrolldog.blogspot.com.

"Go Fetch!"

Austin Rynne PT, DPT

The first time Jake met Bodhi, there were no signs of the bond that was soon to exist between this ten-year-old boy and the energetic Border collie. Jake is autistic and he has difficulty maintaining eye contact and engaging in reciprocal activities with other children or adults. He also has a tendency to self-injure when he becomes upset about something. In this first meeting, Jake barely acknowledged Bodhi or Bodhi's owner, Logan. He spent most of the session standing by the window, staring out into the parking lot,

Jake and Bodhi

and when it was over he just walked out of the room
without saying good-bye.

Over the course of the next several weeks, the relationship between Jake and Bodhi changed dramatically.
I am the Related Services Administrator at the Anderson
Center for Autism in Staatsburg, New York, where I
oversee a variety of therapy programs including speech,
occupational, physical, and music therapies. I also coor-
dinate a dog-assisted therapy program in partnership

with The Good Dog Foundation. Those of us in the autism community have long acknowledged that dogs can help children with autism become more engaged and active participants in the world around them, but seeing this happen firsthand has been incredibly inspiring.

After four or five sessions with Bodhi, there was a striking change in Jake's ability to vocalize what he was thinking and feeling. During the session, Jake's speech therapist, Silka, urged Jake to give Bodhi commands such as "Sit," "Come," and "Walk," and when he did, Bodhi would immediately spring into action. As he witnessed the dog's great enthusiasm, Jake's vocalizing became more and more pronounced and animated. The two began to play fetch with a tennis ball; each time Jake would shout "Go!" and Bodhi bounded across the room to capture his prize, a glowing smile would spread across Jake's face.

Jake has been working with Bodhi for over a year, and the joy he now takes in communicating and socializing with everyone around him is amazing to see. Also, his episodes of engaging in self-injurious behaviors throughout the day have decreased, which means that he is able to focus better in the classroom, thereby improving his overall ability to learn.

These days, when Jake walks through the halls of our school with Bodhi and he encounters friends, he stops, looks them in the eye, and introduces them to his canine friend. And, of course, each time a session with Bodhi is over, Jake's "good-bye" is loud and clear.

Gabriel's Angels

*I have a dog at home and when she was young
I would get really angry, and if I get really angry
I take it out . . . [pause] I take it out on my
dog but now I see I was really wrong. I don't
want to hurt a dog again, they're too lovable.
I just don't want to hurt them again.*

—PETER, AGE 14

When Pam Gaber gets comments and letters like this from the abused and troubled young people she and her volunteers visit with their therapy dogs, it gives her hope that the cycle of violence can be broken. She heads Gabriel's Angels, a nonprofit organization in Arizona that sends out handler-dog therapy teams every week to visit with neglected and at-risk children who have been victims of abuse. As Pam says, "I see the magic that occurs between my dog, Gabriel, and the other dogs and children. Gabriel's Angels is about social change." The children we visit learn to treat animals with love, respect, and compassion—emotions they have had little personal experience with in their own lives.

The magic began in May 2000, when Pam left a twenty-year career in corporate sales in the pharmaceutical industry to dedicate herself to volunteerism. Soon after she made this career change, she adopted a Weimaraner puppy named Gabriel and began to donate time at a crisis center for abused children in Phoenix. Because puppies and children seemed a natural fit, she asked permission to bring Gabriel with her one day to the shelter, and the children, many of whom were normally withdrawn and cautious around her, suddenly became animated when they saw the dog. The excitement that Gabriel's presence generated gave Pam an idea: She could make a positive difference in the lives of these children—and others—if she brought dogs into their world. So Pam started Gabriel's Angels, and she and her puppy went to work.

Ten years later, and with about one hundred therapy teams (dog and owner/volunteer), Gabriel's Angels works tirelessly to rebuild trust, tolerance, and self-esteem among children who are the victims of family violence and sexual abuse. The teams visit domestic abuse shelters, juvenile detention facilities, and other agencies that tend to the needs of troubled young people from infancy to age eighteen.

"The children we visit are victims of violence," says Pam. "Above all, they lack trust. People in their lives have let them down: They've walked out and not come back, they've made promises they didn't keep, and they've hurt the children physically and emotionally. What we do with the dogs is establish trust: We visit these children week after week; the dogs keep coming back. Once we can gain a child's trust, then we can work on giving them the help they need."

Pam soon learned that the simplest comments can mean the most. "One time a young boy named Mark, who was about six years old, shouted 'Bad dog!' at Gabriel. Then the child tried to hit Gabriel while he was sitting quietly on a lead at my side. The counselor explained that the boy had had a bad dog at home and that violence was an everyday occurrence in the family. Over a series of visits I let Mark get comfortable with Gabriel. I explained how Gabriel was like him in some ways, because they both needed food and water and exercise to live. I let Mark listen to Gabriel's heart with a stethoscope and let him hold the leash. After a few weeks, Mark came up to me during one of our visits and said, 'Miss Pam, Gabriel needs some water.' That was a huge step for Mark: He understood that Gabriel was a living, feeling being that needed and deserved comforts. That's the kind of magic I see when I work with these children."

For Pam, the special moments keep coming. One dear to her heart occurred soon after Gabriel's Angels was established. She and Gabriel were visiting a class in a crisis nursery where the children were three to five years old. During their second visit, a wide-eyed four-year-old girl named Natalie walked up to Gabriel and said, "Hi, big gray dog. What's your name?" She didn't wait for Pam to answer, but very confidently took the leash and began to lead Gabriel around the room. Pam followed closely, amused at how this pint-sized child had taken over and impressed by the self-confidence she displayed. Natalie methodically led Gabriel to each of the other twelve children in the room and introduced him to each one, saying, "This is Gabe, he's my friend."

This entire process took close to an hour, as Natalie made it a point to let each child know that she was in charge. It was then time for the children to have their snacks, so Pam explained to Natalie and to all the children that it was time for Gabriel to go home and that they would come back the next week.

The following Tuesday, as Pam and Gabriel walked into the classroom, Natalie ran across the room, shouting, "Gabe came back, Gabe came back!" The other children crowded around as Gabriel became the center of attention. Pam took Natalie's excitement in stride, and it was not until one of the teachers, Deborah, pulled her aside before she and Gabriel left for the day that she learned just how significant it was. Deborah said that the minute Pam and Gabriel had left the classroom the previous week, Natalie loudly announced to the other children that "Gabe isn't coming back. He won't keep his word. He's not coming back." That's when Pam realized that this child had already learned at four years of age how to shield herself from disappointment.

But Gabriel did go back, and kept going back, week after week. Deborah told Pam that the relationship Natalie had with Gabriel was the first trust relationship she had had in her life. "Now she can see that trust is okay, that it doesn't always lead to disappointment." When it came time for Natalie to graduate from preschool and Gabriel—but not Pam—received an invitation to the commencement ceremony, Pam knew she had done her job well. Pam went to the commencement, of course, as Gabriel's "date," and Natalie was beside herself with joy that her friend Gabe had come to her graduation.

Pam and her angels also work with older children: teens in juvenile detention and group homes who have been perpetrators and victims of sexual abuse. Pam has been visiting a group home for teenage boys for about six years, where she and Gabriel show the boys how to do basic obedience trials with the dogs: "Sit," "Stay," "Come," and "Down." Pam notes that performing these training sessions with the dogs gives the boys positive experiences of power.

"When these boys work with a dog, and the dog performs a command as asked, I tell the teens that they need to tell the dog that he's a good boy. I ask them, 'What happens when you do something good? Don't you want to be told you've done a good job?' The thing is, these boys have not had such reassurances in their past. They've had nothing but negative experiences and most likely have never been told that they've done anything good. What their work with the dogs does is, hopefully, make it clear to them that when they have trained the dog to do something and the dog does it, the dog is a 'good boy' and so are they. The boys make a connection with the dogs. And that is critical for these teens, as they have a history of abusing animals."

Pam knows she and her dogs have done a "good job" when they get letters like these from the teen boys:

I get that you learn to respect human's boundaries as well as dog boundaries. You learn to love. That is what I get out of it [Gabriel's Angels visits].
—Andrew, age 14

Why I originally started abusing dogs, was because of all my frustrations. It's like a scapegoat. I would use them to get what I wanted. After . . . ever since doing years of experience with Jack [a therapy dog] and all the other Gabriel's Angels members, I finally get it, and I won't do that again.
—Steven, age 15

And then there are the simple sentiments. When Gabriel had to miss several months of visits because he needed chemotherapy, the children whom he visited made get-well cards and letters for him. The one from five-year-old Jason says it all: "I love him and miss him and I hope he has a good day. When I grow up I'm going to buy him a house and bone."

You can visit Gabriel's Angels at www.gabriels angels.org.

Closing Tails

How Dogs Can Enrich Family Life

This section included stories that celebrated the special relationships that form between children and dogs. The bond between a child and his or her dog, as we have seen, can have lifelong implications. The mere fact that dogs give unconditional love to a child helps shape how that child sees the world and his or her place in it. Several of the stories in this section show this concept in action: "Gabriel's Angels," in which abused and troubled children learn how to give and receive love from dogs, and "Frankie: Keep on Rolling!," in which children learn that it's okay to be different and that what really matters is who you are on the inside rather than on the outside.

Other stories show how a dog in the family can help bring children and parents closer together or, at the very least, allow the child and dog to spend quality time together. In today's hectic society, family life often suffers. One or both parents may need to work long hours or several jobs. Children and parents often don't have meals together, and finding quality time together can be a challenge.

"I often have to work late, until 9 or 10 P.M.," says Chet, an attorney. "Even if I'm home, I'm working in my home office. My two kids play with our two dogs, Moxie and Roxie, and I know where they are and that they're safe. When I'm done working, I can join them. It's a good feeling."

No Dog? No Problem!

If your family does not have a dog but you and your children would like to interact with one or more in some way, there are several things you can do.

- "Borrow" a dog from a friend, family member, or neighbor and volunteer to walk him, take him to the park, or play with him.

- Volunteer at an animal shelter, the Humane Society, or other animal organization in your area. Such facilities typically have age limits for young volunteers, and a parent may be required to accompany the child when he or she is doing volunteer work.

- Participate in a dog reading program. If your child needs help with his or her reading skills, there may be a dog reading program in your area in which you can enroll your child. See section four for a list of organizations that are involved in dog reading programs.

How Dogs Improve Family Dynamics

If your family has a dog now or had one in the past, you may have already realized how important he or she can be in your everyday life. Family researchers and those who work closely with dogs in social environments can back up those feelings. Studies show that more than half of people surveyed who had companion animals said that theirs were of great importance during a family crisis, such as divorce, illness, death, or loss of employment.

The bonds that family members form with their dogs can be very strong, and those bonds can reduce stress and tension in the household and help keep stability in the family.

"It may sound silly, but my dog Roscoe helped me through my divorce," says Paul. "And it really helped the kids as well. Roscoe had been my dog, so he stayed with me. Our kids were only six and eight when Sally and I got divorced, and when I had the kids for visitation, we always did things with the dog. I swear he helped keep us sane. We went to the park, took walks, had picnics, all with Roscoe. The dog was a stabilizing point for the kids and for me."

Having dogs in the family can also help children develop greater self-esteem and self-confidence. It's been shown that young people who feel good about themselves are less likely to be abusive toward people and animals. As evidenced by several stories in this book, children often relate to and communicate things to dogs that they won't with other humans. Thus, dogs can help children develop empathy and nurturing skills.

Dogs are always there to remind us of the importance of playtime.

Families That Play Together Stay Together

One way dogs can improve family dynamics is for family members to become involved in a dog's training and care. Even children as young as four or five can participate in some way. When it's time to take the dog for a walk, for example, a very young child can bring the leash to the family member who will walk the dog. Young children can also help by putting water in the dog's bowl.

All family members may participate in training sessions, whether they are formal (done by a professional trainer either at the house or at a facility) or informal (a program you and your family have chosen to follow). (For information on finding the right training program, see the Resources at the end of this section.) When family members work together to train a dog, the experience promotes cooperation, patience, sharing, and responsibility among the participants. The same is true for sharing responsibilities for the dog's care. Children can be assigned duties that fit their ages and levels of maturity. Some families rotate the duties among the children and the parents, with responsibilities changing every few weeks so everyone gets a chance to provide care and no one has to do a task for very long that he or she doesn't like (picking up dog waste comes to mind).

Even simple activities like walking the dog, taking the dog to a dog park, grooming the dog, or playing with the dog in the yard can be an individual activity or one that several family members can do together.

In the following pages we offer some suggestions, tips, and resources on how children and dogs can safely spend quality time together and form those memorable relationships.

Basic Safety Tips Before Dogs and Kids Play

Children and dogs may go together like peanut butter and jelly, but you still need to practice some caution and follow guidelines to ensure that their interactions are safe. Just as dogs need to be trained to behave and to respond to commands, children need to understand what they can and should not do when they are in the company of a dog, whether it is their own dog or, especially, an unfamiliar one.

"My five-year-old son, Jason, just loves dogs," says his mother, Myra. "Whenever he sees one, he immediately wants to run over and pet it. I learned very quickly that I needed to teach him and constantly reinforce with him that he should not approach a dog without asking me first. When Jason was four years old I turned my back for just a few seconds and he had run over to a Newfoundland and flung his arms around the dog's neck. The dog's owner had her back turned from her dog. Fortunately, Newfoundlands are known for being gentle, but I immediately panicked. Everything was fine, but from that day on I have emphasized with Jason that he must ask me first before he approaches any dog."

To help avoid any accidents or injuries, here are some guidelines to consider before putting children and dogs together.

- Children should be taught to be gentle with a dog and never tease him or her.
- Roughhousing should be discouraged. Such activities encourage biting and other "mouthy" actions by the dog, and the dog may inadvertently hurt the child.
- Good games include fetch, catch, retrieve, hide-and-seek, and the sports activities that are listed under "Activities Kids Can Do with Dogs" (see page 182).
- Children should be taught never to grab toys or other items out of a dog's mouth, or reach into a food bowl or crawl inside a doghouse. Some dogs protect the food, toys, and spaces

that are theirs, and these dogs may snap or
even bite if they feel threatened.

Activities Kids Can Do with Dogs

Games and activities that children and their dogs can
share run a wide range, from games as simple as fetch
to sports activities geared especially toward dogs, such
as agility training and tracking. We have divided the activities into two groups: simple ones that are safe for
young children (but certainly can be done by people of
any age) and more complex activities that may or may
not require formal training and/or team participation.
These latter activities often are represented or supported
by groups or organizations, and we have included contact
information on some of these groups in the Resources
list at the end of this list section so you can investigate on
your own.

EASY ACTIVITIES

These activities can be done regardless of whether
your dog has learned basic commands (e.g., "Sit,"
"Fetch," "Stay," "Down," and "Come"). If the dog has
not yet learned them, the game and the training become

one. Of course, you can always play these games without worrying about the commands.

- Fetch: Use a toy that your dog loves. With your dog on leash, throw the toy a very short distance. Praise your dog enthusiastically if he picks up the toy. Back up to encourage your dog to come toward you with the toy. You can use a treat to trade your dog for the toy if you need to. Start easy and work up to longer distances! Added challenge—encourage your dog to bring the toy right to you and drop it in your hand or at your feet.

- Hide-and-Seek: Have a friend hold your dog while you hide in an easy-to-find place. Excitedly call for your dog. When he finds you, give him lots of praise. Be sure to keep your dog on leash while he and your friend look for you. Added challenge—teach your dog to sit and wait while you hide. Then call him and reward him when he finds you!

- Follow the Leader: Create a small obstacle course in your backyard or an area where you have lots of room to walk. You can use cones, boxes, chairs, or anything that is easy to see and maneuver around. Encourage your dog to walk next to you on leash as you go around one obstacle. Use treats and enthusiastic praise. After you have mastered one obstacle, add in another. Added challenge—work up to walking around all the obstacles with your dog beside you off leash.

MODERATE TO DIFFICULT ACTIVITIES

- Agility: Picture an obstacle course where dogs can walk on balance beams, walk through tunnels, leap over barriers, and maneuver through a maze, and you have an idea of what agility is all about. Agility is a sport that involves close teamwork between the dog and his owner. There are groups that offer training and competition for teens and their dogs. For a list of agility groups and trainers, see www.dogplay.com/Activities/Agility/agilityl.html#findagility.

- Flying Disc: This sport can be simple or more complex. In the simple form, you throw a disc and the dog runs, catches it (he may leap up to do so), and brings it back. If you want to be more creative, you can get involved with competitive flying disc groups and join competitions. Training for disc competition involves patience, skill, and agility. You can learn more at www.dogplay.com/Activities/disc.html.

- Musical Freestyle: Also known as canine freestyle and dog dance, this activity is a combination of obedience and dance. It involves teamwork, rhythm, and coordination. People do it for fun and for competition.

- Obedience Training: Obedience training can mean just simply teaching your dog basic manners, or it can mean competing with your dog in a performance obedience trial in the hope of earning a Novice, Open, or Utility title. Or you can learn the new sport of Rally—which combines parts of traditional obedience exercises and puts them into an agility-style course with numbered signs. Gentle and patient methods of obedience training will strengthen and deepen the bond between you and your dog and your whole family.

- Therapy Dog Programs: Kids and teenagers can participate in some therapy dog programs. Both the training and the therapy visits take much dedication on the part of the dog and its owner. You can learn more about what it takes to be a therapy dog and how to go about participating in therapy dog activities in section four.

- Tracking and Nose Games: Dogs are natural "sniffers," and they love to track and play nose games. For dogs trained for search and rescue or as drug or bomb sniffers, it is "work." Tracking and nose games can be done just for fun, and there are several ideas listed in the Resources to get you started.

The Family and Its Dog

How many times have you heard someone say, "We consider our dog to be part of the family," or "Our dogs are our kids," or "My dog is my baby"? Geraldine, a thirty-nine-year-old mother of three children, says she could not imagine not having a dog. "Scottie is great for the kids. He has helped them learn responsibility, the kids play with him, and my husband and I spend time together walking him. Scottie is definitely a major part of our family."

In the United States, there are approximately 74.8 million dogs who have an owner. Thirty-nine percent of households in the United States own at least one dog, 25 percent own two dogs, and 12 percent have three or more dogs.

You may be among the 61 percent of households that does not own a dog (yet) or you may already have a dog or two but are considering getting another one. In either case, here are some guidelines and suggestions to consider.

How to Choose a Dog for Your Family

Because the dog you select for your family will likely be sharing your living space and time, it is realistic to choose one whose needs, personality, and temperament are most compatible with your lifestyle and family situation. High-rise apartment dwellers in Manhattan may want to think twice about getting a pair of bloodhounds, while someone who wants a dog that will enjoy long hikes in the mountains may want to forgo a dachshund for a more robust dog.

FACTORS TO CONSIDER BEFORE YOU CHOOSE

It's so easy to fall in love with a cuddly puppy and to forget momentarily that the two pounds of fur rolling around at your feet may someday transform into a sixty-pound dog that needs to be exercised several times a day—or one that loves to be a couch potato. Here are some things to consider when choosing a dog for your family.

- Activity Level: All dogs need daily exercise, but some need more than others. Who will be responsible for making sure the dog gets enough exercise each day? Do you live in an area that is safe for walking a dog, one that has dog parks or other opportunities for you to exercise the dog? Do you want a dog that will exercise with you, one that will play with your children in the yard?
- Small Children and Seniors: If you have small children in your home, attention and supervision are paramount for a healthy relationship. Puppies or energetic adult dogs can easily

scratch or knock over a child. Tiny toy-breed puppies or dogs may themselves be injured by an exuberant child. Look for a canine companion who will be gentle and tolerant. For seniors, a calm adult dog with lower exercise requirements can be a suitable choice. Smaller dogs are more easily carried, but if you prefer a larger dog, a greyhound is docile and low energy and could make a lovely companion.

- Other Companion Animals: If you have other animals in the house, you need to consider the impact of introducing a dog to the family. If possible, the new dog should first meet your current companion in a neutral area. Are you hoping the new dog will be a playmate for your other companion animal(s)? Any current companions may resent sharing your attention with a new dog in the house, so you should take steps to make the transition easy.

- Home Environment: Consider the impact the dog will have on your home. Most dogs shed hair, and some breeds shed more than others. Dogs, like children, occasionally have accidents,

such as failure to eliminate outside and vomit-
ing. Will the dog have the run of the house or
be confined to specific areas?

- Outside Environment: Will the dog spend any
  (supervised) time outside? Will you need to get
  a fence or dog run? Consider your landscaping.
  Some dogs like to dig holes in lawns and gar-
  dens. Dog urine can leave yellow patches in
  grass. Dogs and attractive landscaping don't
  have to be mutually exclusive though. See the
  Resources on page 204.

- Your Commitment: Bringing a dog into your
  life is a commitment. Depending on the age of
  the dog when he or she becomes a part of your
  family, that commitment can last ten to fifteen
  years, or even more. Are you considering any
  radical life changes in the future that may prevent you from bringing the dog with you? Obviously, we cannot predict the future, but it is
  wise to put this factor on your list of things to
  consider.

- Puppy or Older Dog: Puppies are cute, but
  they typically require house training, behavior
  training, and supervision to be sure that they

do not chew up your favorite shoes or couch. Think small child with four legs and a need to put everything in his mouth. Puppies require more patience and time commitment.

• Size: Choosing a dog whose adult size fits your lifestyle is important. If you are slight and will be the one to walk the dog, a large, energetic dog will need lots of hours of training walks. When thinking about the size of dog you want, consider the size of your living space, exercise requirements, and even the amount of food you will need to buy.

• Financial Commitment: Having a dog is a financial commitment. We all hope our dogs will live long and healthy lives, and part of that means taking them to the vet for vaccinations and checkups. You will also need to supply food and accessories, such as collars, leashes, bowls, toys, and carriers. Although no one can predict accidents and the development of disease or illness, this possibility should be considered as well. Certain breeds are more prone to genetic problems so you should investigate such information before choosing a dog.

- Purebred or Mixed Breed: Some people prefer purebred dogs because they are attracted to a certain look, or they had that dog as a child, or they want to participate in dog shows. Other people like the idea of adopting a mixed breed dog from a shelter, for reasons listed on pages 193–195.

- Allergies: Allergic reactions to dog dander and/ or saliva are not uncommon. The subject of allergies to dogs received national attention when it was revealed that one of President Obama's daughters has such an allergy. You may want to check with your physician if you suspect anyone in your household may have them.

Where, Oh, Where to Go?

Once you decide you want to get a dog, where should you go to get him? You have several options. Let's look at them for a moment.

SHELTERS AND RESCUE ORGANIZATIONS

Highly recommended and at the top of the list are rescue and adoption organizations and facilities, such as the Humane Society, local county or city dog shelters, gen-

There are millions of homeless dogs waiting in shelters for a family to adopt them and give them a home.

eral dog rescue organizations (those that rescue dogs of any breed), and rescue groups that specialize in specific breeds. From this very broad umbrella of groups you will have many, many choices from which to choose. Why?

There are millions of homeless dogs waiting for a family to adopt them. According to the Humane Society of America, animal shelters care for 6 to 8 million dogs and cats every year in the United States. Approximately 3 to 4 million of them are euthanized. For now, these numbers are estimates because there is no central data reporting agency for animal shelters. About half of the animals taken in by shelters are given up by their owners, and the other half are picked up by animal control agencies. Most of the animals at shelters need new homes because their former owners had unrealistic expectations about the effort, time, and money it takes to maintain a relationship with a companion animal. The vast majority of these animals are healthy and adoptable. All they lack is a loving family, even if it is a family of one.

If your heart is set on a purebred, don't rule out shelters and rescues. Many people do not realize that an estimated 25 percent of dogs given up at shelters are purebred.

"I was really surprised to find a purebred pug at our local animal shelter," says Marcy. "We really had our heart set on a pug, and I was fully prepared to go to a breeder. Then a friend urged me to check with the shelters and rescue organizations. And I'm so glad we did. We found exactly what we wanted!"

If you don't find what you want at an animal shelter, you can check for rescue organizations that specialize in the breed in which you are interested. Search on the Internet, or see the Resources (page 204) for the American Kennel Club's "Breed Rescue Groups" list.

Adopting a Shelter or Rescue Dog

The staff members at animal shelters and rescue organizations have a goal: to make the best adoption matches possible. That's why responsible facilities make every attempt to learn about the history of any animal that is brought to them. Although such information is usually not obtainable when animals are brought in as strays, staff and volunteers can still learn much about them while they are caring for them. Before any animal is put up for adoption—whether he was a stray, was abandoned, or was brought in by a former owner—he is evaluated for health status and temperament.

Advantages of Adopting a
Shelter or Rescue Dog

One warm-and-fuzzy advantage is that you are providing a second (or perhaps third) chance to a dog that needs a loving home. Another is that many shelters provide adoption counseling, dog training classes, behavior counseling, and medical services for new dog owners. The cost of adopting a dog from a shelter is typically less than the cost of buying from a breeder or a pet store. Dogs adopted from shelters have usually been vaccinated, dewormed, and spayed or neutered as well. These services are included in the cost of adoption.

ADVERTISEMENTS: INTERNET AND NEWSPAPERS

Some people advertise on the Internet (e.g., Craigslist, Freecycle) or in newspapers to give away or sell a dog. In many cases, these individuals would rather give their dog to someone they meet face-to-face rather than give him up at a shelter and not know if or when the dog is adopted. If you answer such an ad, you should bring someone with you who can help you evaluate the dog, make observations, and ask questions. Two heads are better than one.

Find out as much as you can about the dog, including vaccination history and health issues. Interact with the dog so you can evaluate his temperament and ability to follow commands. This can be difficult to do. When you go to a shelter or rescue organization, a staff member or trained volunteer will typically go through a procedure with you and the dog to ensure that it is a good fit. Dogs from such organizations typically have also been tested for sociability. Therefore, if you are considering getting a dog from an individual, be sure to take steps to test your compatibility as best you can.

Breeders

We realize there are reputable breeders. But we also recognize the reality of the millions of adoptable homeless dogs who face euthanasia if they do not find a home. We strongly encourage you to investigate your local shelters, rescue organizations, and sanctuaries for your new dog. If you decide to turn to a breeder for your dog, do your research and find a good one. Ask around. If you find a dog you like, ask where he came from. Be sure to meet the parents of the puppy. Ask the breeders if they have health clearances and if they take a dog back at any age and at any time. Ask how many litters a breeder has per year.

What Breed Should You Get?

There are scores of breeds of dogs, but naturally there are ones that are more popular than others. That's not to say that the less popular breeds are not desirable— absolutely not! But each person and each family has different needs and expectations, and each breed of dog has characteristics that are typical for that breed, traits that may be positive or negative, depending on what traits and personality you are looking for.

The ten dog breeds listed here have appeared on various lists of the most popular and suitable dogs for families and/or for friendliness, gentleness, and trainability. Remember, the characteristics listed are general, and you can certainly find these traits in mixed breeds as well.

- Labrador Retriever: These dogs are typically easy to train, make wonderful family companions, and can be excellent sporting dogs as well.
- Golden Retriever: The golden retriever has an excellent temperament, is very affectionate, and is easily trained.
- Boxer: Loyal and affectionate, they are like glue: They like to be with their owners. Great family dogs that need lots of exercise (at least twice a day).
- Cavalier King Charles Spaniel: Happy dogs who love being with you. They are known for being adoring companions and are very trainable. Aggression problems are rare.
- German Shepherd: The German shepherd is known for his intelligence and for being a

working dog (service, police), but makes an excellent family companion as well. Because they are working dogs, they should be with a family that can keep them busy.

- Poodle: This breed is easy to train, is hardy, and seems to readily adapt to any living environment. They are typically very good with children.

- Bernese Mountain Dog: A gentle giant, this breed is great with children of all ages. They are very stable and trainable, and get along with other dogs as well.

- Pug: Wonderful little dogs that love children and all people. They are easygoing and gentle, and they don't need much exercise.

- Collie: Everyone thinks of *Lassie*, and collies do have the same gentle, loving temperament as the dog in the television series. They are great with children.

- Newfoundland: Yes, these dogs are huge, but so very gentle and laid-back that children love them. They are highly trainable and love to be with people.

Labrador retriever

Golden retriever

Cavalier King Charles Spaniel

Boxer

Remember, there are millions of mixed-breed dogs that have wonderful temperaments and personalities.

Now That You've Chosen Your Dog

Once you decide on the dog that will join your household, there are a few things you can do to make the transition as smooth as possible. The following are some activities that can involve the entire family in preparing for your new arrival.

- Accumulate the initial items you will need for the dog, such as bowls, food, collar, leash, and a dog bed.
- Decide which family members will be responsible for different parts of the dog's care: feeding, walking, cleaning up after accidents, and playtime.
- Choose a veterinarian. You might ask friends and relatives who are dog owners for references. Consider location, types of services offered (including emergency services), hours of

operation, number of vets in the practice, and pricing structure.

- Plan to take the dog to a veterinarian as soon as possible for an examination and any needed vaccinations. It is important to establish a relationship with a veterinarian so you and the dog will feel comfortable.

- Emphasize to everyone in the household that it will take some time for the dog and everyone else to adjust to the new situation. Remember that the dog is entering a brand-new environment and may be a bit nervous. Little "accidents" may happen.

- Consider training. The amount of training will depend on the age of the dog and any previous training he may have had. Obedience and lots of other types of fun dog training classes can be a wonderful family activity as well.

Resources

Choosing a Dog

American Kennel Club. "Breed Rescue Groups": www.akc.org/breeds/rescue.cfm

American Veterinary Medical Association. "Pet Selection: What You Should Know About Selecting a Dog": www.avma.org/animal_health/brochures/selecting/dog/selecting_dog_brochure.asp

Best Friends. "Choosing the Right Pet for You": www.bestfriends.org/theanimals/pdfs/allpets/choosingapet.pdf

Dog Breed Info Center. "AKC Recognized Breeds": www.dogbreedinfo.com/a-z.htm

Dog Owner's Guide. "Choosing the Right Dog": www.canismajor.com/dog/tchoose.html

Petfinder.com. "Dog Breeds Guide": www.petfinder.com/dog-breeds

Dogs and Families

"Furry Families: Making a Human-Dog Family through Home." *Social and Cultural Geography* 9, no. 5 (2008): 535–55.

This article highlights three ways that dogs become part of a family and draws on interviews with and diaries recorded by new dog owners in 2006 to 2007.

Guide to Selecting a Behavior Consultant

www.webtrail.com/petbehavior/guide.html

Tips on how to choose a companion animal behavior specialist.

Systemic Solutions: Telephone Coaching and Professional Training

www.soulwork.net/sw_articles_eng/family_pets.htm

Hoover, Lynn. *The Family in Dog Behavior Consulting.* **Orlando, FL: Legard Publishing, 2006.**

Trainer and behavior consultant Lynn Hoover explores the intense and sometimes complicated nature of relationships between families and dogs.

Provides coaching on family companion animals, transference, and relationships. "We can coach you to sort out emotions and relationships about people and pets."

Dogs and Children

"Dogs and Children"

www.cbrrescue.org/articles/kids_and_dogs.htm

An article from Chesapeake Bay Retriever Relief & Rescue on integrating a new dog into a home with children.

"Dogs & Storks"

www.dogsandstorks.blogspot.com.

A program developed by a dog behavior consultant that helps families with newborns and dogs enjoy both with less stress. You can find helpful articles at their blog address listed above.

"Kids and Pets"

www.homevet.com/petcare/kidspets.html

An article from HomeVet that offers guidance on the subject of children and companion animals.

TRAINING

American Dog Trainers Network

www.tonypassera.com/thedogsite/www/new/

Articles and tips on all aspects of dog training.

Association of Pet Dog Trainers

www.apdt.com

A professional association for individual dog trainers.

GAMES AND ACTIVITIES

Canine Freestyle

www.dogdance.net/english_version/definition/definition .html

A comprehensive website that provides information and videos on canine freestyle, also known as musical freestyle or dog dance.

Canine Freestyle Federation, Inc.

www.canine-freestyle.org

Learn all about canine freestyle and see demonstrations on this website.

Dog Scout

www.dogscouts1.com/Dog_Activ-_Scent_Discrim.html

A website with instructions on how to teach and play a series of scent discrimination games with your dog.

Introduction to Scent Discrimination

www.dogscouts.org/Dog_Activ-_Scent_Discrim.html

Several games to teach your dog to use his nose to find the things that you want him to find.

Pawmark

www.pawmark.com/articles/tfields.htm

An article on tracking with your dog.

Alexander, Melissa. *Click for Joy!* Waltham, MA: Sunshine Books, 2003.

Clear and accurate answers for over one hundred commonly asked questions about clicker training in one essential reference. Packed with information that experienced trainers and newcomers alike can put to use immediately.

Coile, D. Caroline. *How Smart Is Your Dog? 30 Fun Science Activities with Your Pet.* New York: Sterling Publishing Co., 2004.

Children can mix play and science with the activities in this book. The different experiments help children test their dog's health, vision, reflexes, and sense of smell, and learn how a dog's life and aging process are different from theirs.

Dog Fancy magazine editors. *Popular Dogs:* *Tricks & Games*. Mission Viejo, CA: Fancy Publications, 2003.

This book offers twenty games, twenty-five activities, and sixty-five tricks to teach your dog. There is also a step-by-step training guide that shows you how to use a clicker to train your dog and practice agility.

Hunter, Roy. *Fun and Games with Dogs*. Eliot, ME: Howln Moon Press, 1993.

Educational and fun games that will teach your dog to enjoy working with you. Improve their performance in obedience and canine sports.

Ludwig, Gerd. *Fun and Games with Your Dog*. Hauppauge, NY: Barron's, 1996.

This manual helps dog owners teach their dogs to run through obstacle courses, play games with balls and Frisbees, jump through hoops, and enjoy other activities.

Rock, Maxine. *Totally Fun Things to Do with Dogs.* New York: John Wiley & Sons, 1998.

Includes games and activities for kids age ten and up and their dogs, such as canine variations on playing catch, fetch, and hide-and-seek, and how to throw parties for your dog. Also includes basic training tips and facts about dogs.

Rosenthal, Lisa. *A Dog's Best Friend Activity Book.* Chicago: Chicago Review Press, 1999.

This book contains more than sixty activities that can help strengthen the relationship between kids and their dogs. Some examples include how to make canine crafts, bake dog biscuits, and plan a doggie birthday party. Also includes tips on obedience training, website listings, a children's reading list, trivia for dog lovers, and more.

Sundance, Kyra. *101 Dog Tricks: Step-by-Step Activities to Engage, Challenge, and Bond with Your Dog.* Gloucester, MA: Quarry Books, 2007.

The largest dog trick book on the market and the only one with full-color photos of each trick and its training steps.

4

getting involved

How to Become a
Handler-Dog
Therapy Team

Tens of thousands of people across the nation work or volunteer with a therapy dog. I have the privilege and honor of working with hundreds of such dedicated individuals through The Good Dog Foundation. As its founder and executive director, I am continually blessed with opportunities to enrich the lives of people of all ages by introducing them to the unconditional love of a therapy dog, whether it be in a hospital, correctional institution, psychiatric facility, elementary school, nursing home, or any other facility where people who have physical, emotional, educational, or spiritual needs can benefit by a visit from a handler-dog therapy team.

Good Dog Jazz visiting Atria Retirement Community
in Riverdale, New York

Teamwork

As wonderful and endearing as therapy dogs are, they are half of a team. When the human halves are asked why they volunteer their time and effort, the most common answers I hear are that it is "tremendously re-warding," that they "get back much more than they give," and that they "love the joy their dog brings to others." These individuals and their dogs go out into the world as teams and share that joy with thousands of people every year.

Many people don't realize that you can't just walk into a hospital, nursing home, or other facility with your dog without first going through some training. The rela-tionship between you, your companion dog, and the people you visit is complex, and there are guidelines and some special skills that you will need to learn before you and your dog can enter a facility. These basic require-ments are necessary to help ensure your own safety, your dog's, and that of the people you visit. All therapy dog organizations have their own guidelines and evaluation requirements that individuals and their dogs must meet in order to be a part of their visiting dog therapy programs. In the following pages I will describe how The Good Dog Foundation prepares dogs and handlers to become teams.

If you live in New York, New Jersey, Connecticut, or Massachusetts and are interested in our training, please take a look at our website, www.thegooddogfoundation .org, and give us a call!

How We Prepare Therapy Dog Teams at The Good Dog Foundation

It's always a thrill for me to see a dog and his handler come to The Good Dog Foundation for the first time to begin their training, and then see them after they have "graduated" as a handler-dog therapy team. There is a transformation that takes place—subtle in some cases, more pronounced in others—as dog and handler seem to be more aware of and move in sync with each other, truly working as a team.

As you travel the road to becoming a therapy dog team, here are some things you can do to prepare yourself and your dog for therapy visits:

- Socialize and socialize more. Does your dog seem eager to get attention and affection from all kinds of new people? Notice how your dog responds to a wide range of people, from toddlers and teens to people with beards, people wearing uniforms, or people in wheelchairs.

- Obedience training. Does your dog respond to your cues reliably when asked to do so? It is of utmost importance that a therapy dog is calm and controlled enough to pay attention and react quickly according to your instruction in any situation. This guarantees safe visits for everyone. Find a reward-based class or trainer in your area. There is no room for harshness or punishment in therapy training or work.

- Acclimate to new and unusual environments. Does your dog behave in a calm and relaxed manner when you take him to new places? Therapy dogs need to be relaxed around crowds, loud noises, hospital equipment, slippery floors, and other animals.

- Volunteer on your own at a facility such as a hospital or day program. Find out whether you enjoy talking to and helping people. If you love it, adding your dog to the mix is the easy part!

The Good Dog Foundation's Program

The Good Dog Foundation offers a thorough evaluation, training program, and follow-up program for its Good Dog therapy teams. The Foundation initially evaluates a handler and his or her dog as a team to determine which level class they are placed in. Good Dog offers fundamental obedience, basic obedience, and therapy dog classes. If the handler-dog team passes the class and become certified, they are completely supported by The Good Dog Foundation staff.

Here are more details on how The Good Dog Foundation program works.

INITIAL EVALUATION SESSION

To ensure that a dog and his handler have at least the potential to succeed in the program, they must undergo a brief (about fifteen-minute) evaluation session conducted by a Good Dog trainer. During this session, the

Good Dog Shadow works with Shaun at the Anderson Center for Autism to help him develop communication skills.

trainer observes a dog's personality, energy level, and sociability (with people and with other dogs), as well as the handler's relationship with and basic control of the dog.

The trainer then recommends one of the following courses of action for the potential volunteer handler-dog team:

- Join the Good Dog Foundation Fundamental Training and Evaluation Course—four sessions

- Join the Good Dog Foundation Basic Training and Evaluation Course—four sessions
- Join the Good Dog Foundation Therapy Dog Training and Evaluation Course—five sessions
- Seek out additional training first, which will give your dog more time to mature, and return for an evaluation at a later date
- Consider an alternative activity for which your dog's temperament may be better suited

When a trainer recommends the last option, it may be because the dog displays one or more of the following behaviors and/or conditions that are not compatible with therapy dog service:

- Aggression toward people
- Aggression toward other dogs
- Obvious signs of fearfulness or shyness
- Urinating or defecating indoors
- Overexcitability (e.g., excessive barking, licking, and wiggliness; jumping up on people; mouthing; or pawing)
- Advanced age
- Medical concerns

The Good Dog Foundation trainers also observe some human behaviors that are incompatible with therapy dog service. These include:

- Abusive or rough handling of the dog
- A non-nurturing nature
- Harsh or punishing training methods
- Unwillingness to take direction from Good Dog Foundation trainers
- Lack of attention to the dog's behavior in his surroundings

The Good Dog Foundation's trainers recognize that dogs, like people, may perform better or worse on a test on any given day, and that behavior is not constant and immutable. That's why The Good Dog Foundation's total evaluation process is based on performance throughout the training course, not just on a single test. For the duration of the training sessions, the dogs are exposed to many different people and stimuli with which they can become increasingly confident. This process ultimately leads to consistently safe and enjoyable visits for the clients, handlers, and dogs alike.

TRAINING AND EVALUATION COURSES

We have developed a highly effective multiple-session training course for dogs that uses positive reinforcement and patient, reward-based methods. One of the many advantages to this approach is that gentle, loving dogs that may have a temporary problem with manners because they are nervous or excited at first are not summarily excluded from participating in our therapy-dog-services work.

Here is a summary of what is included in each of the Good Dog Foundation training programs. Although the Fundamental and Basic Dog Training courses are similar, the Fundamental Dog Training course is geared especially for dogs who have no prior training.

Fundamental Dog Training:
Four one-hour sessions
- Basic obedience ("Sit," "Down," "Stay," walk on a loose lead)
- Relaxation and control

Basic Dog Training: Four one-hour sessions
- Basic obedience ("Sit," "Down," "Stand," "Stay," walk on a loose lead)

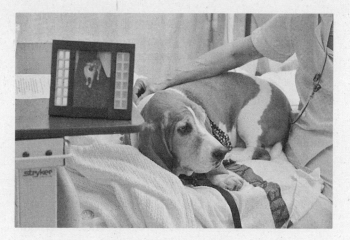

Good Dog Agatha visiting with a patient at New York Presbyterian Hospital, Manhattan.

- Begin gentling exercises and desensitization to handling and novel stimuli
- Begin familiarization with hospital equipment
- Socialization exercises with other dogs and people

Therapy Dog Training:

Five one-hour sessions

- Meeting and greeting exercises
- Familiarization with hospital equipment

- Role-playing for hospital environment
- Instruction and coaching on safe dog-handling in health care facilities

FOLLOW-UP SUPPORT

Our volunteers are the lifeblood of the Foundation: Without them we would not be able to provide the services that we do. That's why, once handler-dog teams become certified, The Good Dog Foundation staff continually supports and encourages our volunteers to ensure they have the most rewarding and enjoyable experiences possible.

For example, the Foundation staff maintains a close relationship with each of the facilities that our handler-dog therapy teams serve, so our teams always feel welcome and secure wherever they go. We assess and work with each team to help handlers select the places they would like to visit. Our experienced handler-dog teams always "buddy up" and accompany new teams on their first walk-through of the facility they have chosen.

Volunteers are always welcome to ask questions and get assistance from the Foundation's professional peer support groups. The Good Dog Foundation also holds

events each year that recognize volunteers for their service in all the regions served by the Foundation.

Therapy Dogs and Children

One of the most popular activities that handler-dog
therapy teams participate in is reading programs for children. It is certainly a big hit with The Good Dog Foundation dog teams! Two of the stories in this book talk
about such a program: "Reading—Going to the Dogs"
and "Hooch," both in section one. Because so many
people want to learn more about this program and the
role dogs can have in the classroom that we have included
a section about it here.

Children Reading to Dogs

Children have probably been reading to their dogs for
decades, but the concept of a formalized program in
which therapy dogs and their handlers meet with children is only about a decade old. Credit for the birth of
such a program is usually given to Intermountain Ther-

apy Animals of Salt Lake City, Utah, which launched
READ (Reading Education Assistance Dogs) in 1999,
the first comprehensive literacy program based on children reading to dogs. Today there are hundreds of READ
programs throughout the country in schools, libraries,
and other places where children and dogs can meet and
read. The Good Dog Foundation is proud to partner with
many schools and libraries, and I'm happy to report that
these reading programs are extremely successful. Similar
reading programs also operate under different names,
but they all strive to achieve the same general goals,
namely:

- Improving the literary skills of children who
  have poor reading skills with the help of certified handler-dog therapy teams
- Enhancing the self-esteem of these children
  through the process of improving their reading
- Teaching children how to interact with animals

Research shows that children who have low self-
esteem are often more willing to interact with an animal
than with a person, because the animal is less intimidat-

Good Dog Max Freeman listens attentively at a reading program at P.S. 96 in Manhattan.

ing and does not pass judgment. Children who participate in these programs not only improve their reading
abilities, they also tend to become much more enthusiastic readers who actively seek out books, improve their
performance in school, and discover that learning can
be fun.

Dogs in the Classroom

In some special education and regular classrooms
around the United States, certified therapy dogs provide
social support and have been shown to motivate students
to learn and to invite peer interaction. Therapy dogs are
used by social workers, therapists, and early-education
and special-needs teachers who work with children who
have physical, emotional, and developmental disabilities.

Therapy dogs in educational settings are popping up
all around the United States. Here are just a few of the
places where these canines are helping children learn.

- Palmyra-Macedon High School in Wayne
  County, New York, which has a district of
  about 2,200 students. That's where Morgan, a
  golden retriever and poodle mix, is just one of

seven therapy dogs who help the kids feel more confident about their reading and writing skills, concentrate on their schoolwork, and de-stress.

- The Evanlake Cavaliers of New Jersey, which launched the Canine Assisted Resources in Education (CARE) program in 2002. After a very successful pilot program in the Preschool Disability Program in Knowlton, New Jersey, the program took off. Therapy dogs and their volunteer handlers regularly visit special education classrooms throughout the district and are happy to report "the small miracles that happen at almost every visit."

- The Canine Assistance Rehabilitation Education and Services (CARES) program of Concordia, Kansas, which has trained more than 750 dogs since its inception in 1994. The dogs are sent to classrooms throughout the United States, Puerto Rico, and even Peru. See the Resources at the end of this section.

- The Heartland Bernese Mountain Dog Club, which provides therapy dogs for children in reading programs and special education classes, and for other special educational needs in Kansas, Nebraska, Iowa, Missouri, Oklahoma, and Arkansas.

- Kingsbridge International High School in the Bronx, New York. Principal Ron Newlon and his Good Dog Foundation therapy dog, Max, work on English with newly emigrated students who have oftentimes never seen a dog in their lives.

Therapy dogs in the classroom can help teach children a variety of skills beyond improving reading ability. For example, dogs help children:

- Learn how to ask for help. Children are more willing to approach people, including authority figures (e.g., teachers, administrators) who have dogs.
- Control their behavior. Children see that the dogs behave in the classroom, so they learn to display the same behavior as well.
- Improve their memory skills. Children can learn a series of commands when they interact with the dogs.

- Build a positive relationship with animals. Learning to respect and empathize with animals early in life is important, as it discourages animal abuse.
- Attain a higher IQ. Research shows that children who have regular contact with animals have a higher IQ.

Resources

There are many excellent dog therapy programs and organizations across the United States. Below are a few groups representing different parts of the country, as well as other information relating to how you can become involved with therapy dogs.

The Apple

http://theapple.com/topics/2765-therapy-dogs/posts

A forum where teachers meet and discuss the use of therapy dogs in the classroom.

Evanlake Cavaliers

http://evanlakecavaliers.com/therapy.htm

A pet therapy group that sends its certified Cavalier King Charles spaniels to classrooms as part of its Canine Assisted Resources in Education (CARE) program.

The Good Dog Foundation

www.thegooddogfoundation.org

Heartland Bernese Mountain Dog Club

www.hbmdc.org/TherapyDogs.html

Established in 1990, the Heartland Bernese Mountain Dog Club (HBMDC) provides therapy dogs for children in reading programs, special education classes, and other special educational needs, as well as for nursing homes and other therapeutic settings. Therapy dogs from HBMDC serve Kansas, Nebraska, Iowa, Missouri, Oklahoma, and Arkansas.

Intermountain Therapy Animals

www.therapyanimals.org/read

The nonprofit organization that launched the READ program in 1999.

**"Therapy Dog Helps Educators
Connect with Kids"**

www.westbranchtimes.com/article.php?id=3819

An article on the success enjoyed by educators and children in West Branch, Iowa, and their therapy dog from CARES of Concordia, Kansas.

**"Lessons: For a Boy Stumbling Over Words,
a Dog Is the Ideal Reading Partner"**

http://query.nytimes.com/gst/fullpage.html?res=9A06EFD F1230F933A25752C0A9619C8B63

An article from *The New York Times*, January 10, 2007.

Books

Jasheway, Leigh Ann. *Bedtime Stories for Dogs*. Kansas City, MO: Andrews McMeel Publishing, 1996.

A hilarious volume for dogs and their human parents.

Miller, Sara Swan. *Three Stories You Can Read to Your Dog*. Boston, MA: Sandpiper, 1997.

Children ages four through eight can share these short, easy-to-read stories with their dogs.

Miller, Sara Swan. *Three More Stories You Can Read to Your Dog*. Boston, MA: Sandpiper, 2001.

More great stories for kids ages four through eight to read to their dogs.

Acknowledgments

I could not have written this book had it not been for the beautiful gifts of so many caring and loving dogs throughout my life and the lives of many. I want to thank them for their continued unconditional love, support, and healing.

I have many people to thank for their hard work and dedication to this book: Lynn Sonberg, Book Producer, offered the creative vision for this book; Sara Carder, Executive Editor at Penguin Group, provided beautiful editing and guidance throughout the process;

Brianna Yamashita, Associate Director of Publicity at Penguin Group, created an exciting promotional campaign; Susy Nastasi, Director of Field Operations and Training for The Good Dog Foundation, imparted her expertise in training suggestions and insightful resources along with her countless hours of dedication to making this book a reality; Clarissa Gonzalez, Public Relations Consultant for The Good Dog Foundation, spent many hours helping me behind the scenes with this book; Kathy Landman, photographer, provided inspirational photos of Good Dogs helping heal humans and has supported The Good Dog Foundation throughout the years; and Michael Nastasi, who also shared his touching photos to make this book as beautiful as it is.

My father's love of animals started me on this journey of understanding the special gifts they share. He holds a special place in my heart. My love and appreciation for my husband, Patrick McMullan, cannot be measured. His love, devotion, and continued support have helped me for so many years throughout the creation of The Good Dog Foundation and during this book project. I offer a special thank-you to my two children, Pace and Izzy, whose constant love and care give me sunshine

ACKNOWLEDGMENTS

each day. They helped my creative process flow during this project and every day of my life.

Finally, I would like to thank all the people who contributed their stories and photos to the pages of this book. Without these beautiful stories of the gifts these dogs have given, this book could never have been written.

PHOTO CREDITS

Pages xv, 43, 214, 223: © Kathy Landman 2009. All rights reserved. Cannot be reproduced without written permission.

Pages 5, 9, 12: courtesy Claire Vaccaro

Page 17: courtesy Corrie Russinko

Pages 25, 227: © Andrew Yackira 2009. All rights reserved. Cannot be reproduced without written permission.

Page 31: courtesy Daniel Simone

Page 49: courtesy Sharan Wilson, Freedom Service Dogs, Inc.

Pages 51, 54, 66, 70, 73: courtesy Kati Rule, Autism Service Dogs of America

Page 78: courtesy Alison Dolan

Page 84: courtesy Artie Guerrero

Page 99: courtesy Becky Blanton

Page 108: courtesy Debbie Jacobs

Page 127: courtesy Sassafras Lowrey

PHOTO CREDITS

Pages 134, 193, 200, 201: © Michael Nastasi 2009. All rights reserved. Cannot be reproduced without written permission.

Page 158: courtesy Barbara Techel

Page 163: courtesy Susan Trevor

Page 178: © Susy Nastasi 2009. All rights reserved. Cannot be reproduced without written permission.

Page 219: courtesy Roseann & Frank McCann, Anderson Center for Autism

INDEX

INDEX

INDEX

If you enjoyed this book, visit

www.tarcherbooks.com

and sign up for Tarcher's e-newsletter to receive
special offers, giveaway promotions, and
information on hot upcoming releases.

TARCHER
PENGUIN

Great Lives Begin with Great Ideas

New at **www.tarcherbooks.com**
and **www.penguin.com/tarchertalks**:

Tarcher Talks, an online video series featuring
interviews with bestselling authors on everything from creativity and prosperity to 2012
and Freemasonry

If you would like to place a bulk order
of this book, call 1-800-847-5515.

Send Us Your
Inspiring Dog Tales

Enter our contest for a chance to have your story published in the next edition of *Every Dog Has a Gift*.

Just as every dog has a gift, we also believe every dog owner has a story. We're looking for a few good dog tales. If the stories in this book have brought back memories of your own dog, we'd like to read your personal dog story. It can be funny or heartwarming but, like the stories in *Every Dog Has a Gift*, it should also be a true tale that highlights how your dog or dogs have impacted your life.

The deadline for story submissions is June 18, 2010. Individual stories (you can enter as many as you'd like) should be no more than 2,000 words. For complete guidelines and to enter your story, visit www.penguin.com/everydog.